I DIDN'T GET TO SAY GOODBYE
HEALING AFTER THE SUDDEN DEATH OF A LOVED ONE (A GRIEF RECOVERY BOOK)

JEFFREY SIMMONS

SIMMONS ENTERPRISES

© **Copyright Jeffrey Simmons 2024 - All rights reserved.**

The content within this book may not be reproduced, duplicated or transmitted without direct written permission from the author or the publisher.

Under no circumstances will any blame or legal responsibility be held against the publisher or author for any damages, reparation, or monetary loss due to the information contained within this book. Either directly or indirectly. You are responsible for your own choices, actions, and results.

Legal Notice:

This book is copyright protected. This book is only for personal use. You cannot amend, distribute, sell, use, quote or paraphrase any part, of the content within this book, without the consent of the author or publisher.

Disclaimer Notice:

Please note the information contained within this document is for educational and entertainment purposes only. All effort has been expended to present accurate, up-to-date, and reliable, complete information. No warranties of any kind are declared or implied. Readers acknowledge that the author is not engaging in the rendering of legal, financial, medical or professional advice. The content within this book has been derived from various sources. Please consult a licensed professional before attempting any techniques outlined in this book.

By reading this document, the reader agrees that under no circumstances is the author responsible for any losses, direct or indirect, which are incurred as a result of the use of the information contained within this document, including, but not limited to, — errors, omissions, or inaccuracies.

CONTENTS

Introduction	7
1. Understanding Grief and Its Many Faces	11
2. Navigating Daily Life Amid Grief	27
3. Coping Mechanisms and Emotional Support	41
4. Real-Life Stories and Testimonials	57
5. Legal and Financial Guidance	73
6. Helping Children Cope with Grief	91
7. Cultural and Spiritual Perspectives on Grief	107
8. Moving Forward and Finding Hope	125
Conclusion	143
References	147

This book is inspired by and dedicated to my late fiancée, Brittney Smalley, who passed away on Father's Day, 2018. I am immensely grateful for the three years we shared and the memories we created together. These memories have become my source of strength. Fly high, my beloved; I love you.

Christmas 2015

INTRODUCTION

On Father's Day, June 17, 2018, I returned home from work to a scene that would forever change the course of my life—I discovered my fiancée's lifeless body on the bed. She was the epitome of youth and vitality, recently battling what seemed to be a flu-like illness. Despite a visit to the Emergency Room and subsequent release, nothing had prepared me for this outcome. The shock hit me like a wave, leaving me gasping for air. I remember sitting in my living room, unable to comprehend the reality of the loss. The world seemed to tilt, and a deep, aching void settled in my chest. That moment marked the beginning of a journey I had never anticipated, one filled with grief, confusion, and an overwhelming sense of unfinished business.

If you are reading this, you, too, have faced the sudden loss of someone dear to you. I want to start by acknowledging the depth of your pain. Losing a loved one is always hard, but when it happens unexpectedly, it can feel unbearable. The emotions you are experiencing are valid. Confusion, anger, and sorrow are all part of this challenging journey. This book is a safe space for you to explore these feelings, and you are not alone.

This book aims to help you navigate the complex path of grief after the sudden death of a loved one. It provides practical advice, emotional support, and a sense of community. Through these pages, I hope to offer you the tools and understanding needed to cope with your loss. The journey of grief is unique for each person, and this book is designed to meet you where you are.

Sudden loss brings with it unique challenges. The shock of unexpected news can leave you feeling numb and disoriented. There are often unanswered questions and a sense of unfinished business that can haunt you. Life as you knew it changes in an instant, and the future feels uncertain. This book will address these specific struggles, offering guidance on managing sudden loss's immediate aftermath and long-term impact.

The book is structured to support you through different stages of your grief journey. In the first chapters, we will explore the initial shock and disbelief that follow sudden loss. We will discuss the importance of allowing yourself to feel and express your emotions. Later chapters will delve into making sense of your grief, finding ways to honor your loved one, and gradually moving forward. Throughout the book, you will find personal stories, practical tips, and expert advice to guide you.

As I navigated through the depths of my grief following Brittney's passing, I immersed myself in extensive research on healing and connected with others who had traversed the dark valleys of loss. This book is the culmination of that journey. While the stories shared within these pages are rooted in truth, names and specific details have been altered to safeguard privacy.

My motivation for writing this book comes from a deep passion for helping others heal. Over the years, I have seen many individuals face sudden loss and the profound impact it can have on their lives. My own experiences with grief have shaped my understanding and fueled my desire to offer support. I want you to know that I genuinely care about your journey and am here to help you find a path to healing.

I encourage you to engage with this book actively. Reflect on your experiences, journal your thoughts, and participate in the suggested activities. Your involvement is crucial for your healing process. Grief is not something you passively endure; it is something you actively work through. By engaging with the material, you will find ways to process your emotions and begin to heal.

As you read this book, remember that the journey of grief is not linear. There will be good days and bad days, and that is okay. Healing takes time, and it is important to be patient and compassionate with yourself. Allow yourself to feel whatever comes up; know it is all part of the process. There is no right or wrong way to grieve.

I want to offer you a promise of hope and healing. While this journey will be challenging, you will find support, understanding, and practical tools within these pages. Grief may feel overwhelming now, but with time and effort, you will find a way to move forward. There is a path through this pain, and you are not alone. Together, we will navigate this journey and find a way to honor your loved one while finding peace for yourself.

Thank you for allowing me to be part of your healing journey. Let us take this first step together.

CHAPTER 1
UNDERSTANDING GRIEF AND ITS MANY FACES

When Brittney passed away suddenly, I found myself engulfed in a whirlwind of emotions—shock, disbelief, and an overwhelming sense of emptiness. I remember sitting alone in my room, staring at the walls, feeling like my world had been torn apart. It was then that I realized how profound and all-encompassing grief could be. This chapter aims to help you understand the nature of grief, how it manifests, and how it differs from mourning. We will explore the universal yet highly individual experience of grief and touch on the concept of complicated grief.

THE NATURE OF GRIEF: AN OVERVIEW

Grief is an intense emotional response to loss. It is an inevitable part of life, yet its impact can be devastating. Grief can manifest in various ways, affecting you physically, emotionally, and mentally. Emotionally, you might experience profound sadness, anger, or guilt. These feelings can come in waves or hit you unexpectedly. Physically, grief can take a toll on your body. You might feel fatigued, struggle with insomnia, or notice changes in your appetite. Your body might feel heavy, and you could experience aches and pains without clear medical cause. Mentally, grief can cloud your thoughts. You might find it difficult to concentrate, feel confused, or forgetful. Once simple tasks can seem overwhelming.

Grief and mourning are often used interchangeably, but they are not the same. Grief is the internal experience of loss—your personal and private pain. Mourning, on the other hand, is the outward expression of that grief. It is how you show your grief to the world and adapt to the loss. Cultural and religious traditions can influence mourning. For example, some cultures have specific rituals, like wearing black clothing or holding memorial services, to help people express their grief. Personal expressions of mourning can also vary widely. Some people find comfort in solitude, while others seek the support of family and friends. Mourning is a way to process grief and begin to heal.

Grief is a universal experience, yet it is also profoundly personal. While everyone experiences grief at some point, how you grieve is unique. No two people grieve the same way, even if they have lost the same person. Your relationship with the deceased, your personality, and your life experiences all shape how you grieve. For example, an adult who loses a parent might grieve differently than a child who loses a sibling. Even within the same family, each member's grief can look different. Research shows that while there are common patterns in grief, such as the initial shock and eventual acceptance, the journey is unique for everyone.

Complicated grief is a term used to describe a prolonged and intense form of grief that interferes with daily life. While it is normal for grief to be intense and painful, complicated grief persists longer and can be more debilitating. Symptoms of complicated grief can include persistent longing for the deceased, difficulty accepting the death, and an inability to move on with life. If you find that your grief is not easing over time or if it affects your ability to function, it may be time to seek professional help. Grief counselors and therapists can provide support and strategies to help you cope with your loss.

Understanding the nature of grief is the first step in navigating your own experience. It is important to recognize that your feelings are valid and that there is no right or wrong way to grieve. Grief is a deeply personal and unique experience, and it is okay to feel whatever you are feeling. This chapter aims to provide you with a better understanding of what grief is and how it can affect you. By understanding the nature of grief, you can begin to find ways to cope and heal.

THE STAGES OF GRIEF: A NON-LINEAR EXPERIENCE

The stages of grief, introduced by Elisabeth Kübler-Ross in her groundbreaking work "On Death and Dying," offer a framework for understanding the emotional landscape following a loss. These stages—denial, anger, bargaining, depression, and acceptance—are not rigid steps but rather common responses that many people experience. Denial often comes first, a protective mechanism that cushions the initial shock. You might think, "This can't be happening," or feel numb as if the world around you has become surreal. It's a way for your mind to give you time to absorb the reality of the loss.

Anger follows, and it can feel intense and consuming. You might direct it at yourself, the deceased, or even the situation that caused the loss. This anger is a natural part of grieving, an emotional release that can sometimes feel overwhelming. Bargaining is the stage where you find yourself making deals or thinking of "what if" scenarios. You might catch yourself wishing you could turn back time or change the outcome, even though you know it's impossible. This stage reflects a struggle to regain control in a situation where you feel powerless.

Depression sets in as the reality of the loss becomes undeniable. This stage is marked by profound sadness and a sense of emptiness. You might feel that life has lost meaning, and everyday tasks become burdensome. It's a period of deep reflection and sorrow where the weight of the loss truly sinks in. Acceptance, the final stage, doesn't mean you're "over" the loss. Instead, it signifies a gradual adjustment to life without your loved one. You begin to find ways to move forward while still cherishing memories. Acceptance allows you to integrate the loss into your life, finding a new sense of normalcy.

However, it's crucial to understand that these stages are not linear. You might find yourself moving back and forth between them or experiencing multiple stages at once. For instance, you might feel anger one day and slip back into denial the next. This non-linear progression is perfectly normal. I remember speaking with a friend who lost his father. He shared how he would feel a sense of acceptance one moment, only to be hit by a wave of sadness and bargaining the next. This oscillation between stages is a common part of grieving.

Alternative models also offer valuable insights into the grieving process. The Dual Process Model, for instance, suggests that people oscillate between confronting their grief and engaging in restorative activities. One day, you might find yourself deeply immersed in memories and sorrow, while another day, you might focus on work or hobbies to find relief. This model highlights the balance between facing grief and taking breaks from it. Similarly, Worden's Tasks of Mourning outlines four tasks: accepting the reality of the loss, processing the pain of grief, adjusting to a world without the deceased, and finding an enduring connection with the loved one while moving forward. These tasks provide a practical approach to navigating grief.

Emotional oscillation is another aspect to consider. It's the process of moving between confronting grief and seeking respite from it. You might find yourself deeply immersed in sorrow, only to shift your focus to a distraction or a comforting activity. This oscillation is a natural coping mechanism, allowing you to manage the intensity of your emotions. Research supports this, showing that people who oscillate between grief and restorative activities often cope better in the long run.

Grief is not a straightforward path. It's a complex, non-linear experience that varies from person to person. While frameworks like the stages of grief can provide guidance, it's important to remember that your journey is unique. Understanding the fluid nature of these stages and models can help you navigate your grief with greater compassion for yourself.

GRIEF AFTER LOSING A SPOUSE (OR LIFE PARTNER)

Losing a spouse is one of the most profound and life-altering experiences one can endure. The person you planned to share your days with, from mundane routines to grand adventures, is suddenly gone. This loss shatters not only your heart but also your sense of identity. You might find yourself grappling with the loss of shared dreams and plans. The future you envisioned together—growing old, celebrating milestones, supporting each other through thick and thin—feels like a distant, unreachable fantasy. The void left by your spouse can make the world seem colorless and the days feel endless.

Changes in social status and identity are another harsh reality of losing a spouse. Suddenly, you are no longer part of a couple. Social gatherings that once felt comfortable may now feel awkward or even painful. Friends may not know how to interact with you, and you might feel like an outsider in spaces where you once belonged. Your identity, intertwined with that of your spouse, now feels fragmented. You may struggle with the question, "Who am I without them?" The roles you played together—partner, confidant, co-pilot—are now roles you must navigate alone.

The emotional and physical impacts of losing a spouse are profound. Loneliness and isolation can be overwhelming. The silence in the house, the empty side of the bed, and the absence of someone to share your thoughts with can amplify your sense of loss. Emotionally, you may feel a rollercoaster of feelings, from deep sorrow to resentment and sometimes even guilt. Physically, the stress of grief can manifest in various ways. You might experience fatigue, insomnia, or physical aches and pains. Your immune system may weaken, making you more susceptible to illness. These physical symptoms are your body's way of expressing the deep emotional pain you are enduring.

Coping with the loss of a spouse requires finding new ways to navigate daily life and seeking support. Joining support groups for widows and widowers can provide a sense of community and understanding. You can share your experiences with others who truly understand your pain in these groups. Rebuilding a daily routine is also crucial. Establishing new habits and finding activities that comfort you can help create a sense of normalcy. These small steps can make a significant difference, whether it's a morning walk, a new hobby, or volunteering.

One person I spoke with, Jane, lost her husband unexpectedly. She shared how joining a support group for widows helped her navigate the initial shock and loneliness. "It was a lifeline," she said. "Being around others who had experienced the same loss made me feel less alone." Jane also emphasized the importance of rebuilding her daily routine. She started gardening, a hobby she had always wanted to try. "It gave me something to look forward to each day," she explained. "It was a small way to bring some life back into my world."

Another story comes from Mark, who found solace in writing letters to his late wife. "I would write to her every day," he said. It helped me process my emotions and feel connected to her." Mark also joined a local hiking group, which provided physical exercise and social interaction. "Being in nature and meeting new people was incredibly healing," he shared.

These real-life testimonials highlight the diverse ways individuals cope with the loss of a spouse. While the pain never fully disappears, finding support and rebuilding daily routines can help you navigate this difficult chapter. Each person's path to healing is unique, and there is no right or wrong way to grieve. Whether through support groups, new hobbies, or personal rituals, finding what works for you is key. Remember, seeking help and taking small steps toward healing is okay.

GRIEF AFTER LOSING A CHILD

Losing a child is a grief that defies description, shaking the very foundation of your existence. It's a unique kind of pain that reverberates through every aspect of your life. The loss of future milestones—birthdays, graduations, weddings—becomes an agonizing reminder of what will never be. Each missed milestone is like a fresh wound, reopening the grief you thought you had begun to heal from. The dreams you had for your child's future are abruptly shattered, and the world feels profoundly out of order. This disruption extends beyond your own heart; it impacts your entire family dynamic. Siblings may struggle to understand why their brother or sister is no longer there, and spouses may grieve differently, leading to emotional distance. The family unit, once a source of comfort, can become a complicated landscape of individual grief paths.

The emotional complexities of losing a child are intense and multifaceted. Guilt often takes center stage, as parents question every decision they made—wondering if there was anything they could have done differently. This guilt can be paralyzed, leading to an endless loop of "what ifs" and self-recrimination. Anger is another powerful emotion, sometimes directed inward, sometimes at others, or even at the universe itself. The profound sadness that accompanies this loss can feel insurmountable, a heavy weight pressing down on your very soul. You may cry at unexpected moments or feel a hollowness that seems impossible to fill. These emotions are natural and valid, but they can also be overwhelming.

Coping with the loss of a child requires finding ways to honor their memory while navigating your own grief. Memorializing your child can be a deeply healing act. Creating a memory box, planting a tree, or even establishing a scholarship in their name can provide a sense of ongoing connection. Engaging in advocacy or volunteer work related to causes your child cared about can also offer a way to channel your grief into positive action. These acts of remembrance honor your child and create a legacy that keeps their spirit alive.

I remember a mother who lost her teenage son in a car accident. She found solace in organizing charity runs to raise awareness about road safety. "It gave me a purpose," she said, "a way to make sure his death wasn't in vain." Another parent who lost a young daughter to illness shared how creating a garden in her memory became a sanctuary for the family. "Every flower we plant feels like a tribute to her life," she explained. These stories highlight the variety of ways parents find to cope with their immense loss.

Support groups can be an invaluable resource during this time. Connecting with other parents who have experienced similar losses can provide a sense of understanding and community. Groups like The Compassionate Friends and Bereaved Parents of the USA offer both online and in-person meetings where you can share your story and hear from others who truly understand your pain. These groups provide emotional support and practical advice on navigating the many challenges of such a profound loss.

Here are some support groups that may be helpful:

Support Groups for Parents Who Have Lost a Child

- **The Compassionate Friends**: Offers support groups nationwide and online resources for bereaved parents, grandparents, and siblings.
- **Bereaved Parents of the USA**: Provides local chapter meetings and a national conference to support grieving families.
- **GriefShare**: A faith-based support group that offers seminars and support for those who have lost a loved one.
- **MISS Foundation**: Focuses on providing support and resources for parents enduring the loss of a child.

These resources can offer a sense of community and shared understanding, helping to alleviate the isolation that often accompanies this kind of loss. Remember, you don't have to navigate this painful path alone. Seeking support and finding ways to honor your child can be crucial steps in your healing process.

GRIEF AFTER LOSING A PARENT

Losing a parent is a profound experience that can shake your sense of security and alter the very structure of your family. The person who provided guidance and support throughout your life is suddenly gone, leaving a void that seems impossible to fill. This loss can bring about a deep sense of vulnerability. You may find yourself grappling with the realization that the safety net you always relied on is no longer there. The sense of stability and comfort that your parent provided is irreplaceable, and their absence can make the world feel like a less certain place.

Beyond the emotional impact, the loss of a parent can lead to significant changes in family roles and responsibilities. You might find yourself stepping into new roles you hadn't anticipated, such as becoming the family matriarch or patriarch. Sibling dynamics can shift as everyone adjusts to the new family structure. Managing the household, making important decisions, and caring for other family members may fall on your shoulders. These changes can be overwhelming, adding another layer of stress to your grief.

Emotionally, the loss of a parent can bring a range of feelings, including grief and regret over unresolved issues. You may reflect on past conversations, wishing you had said or done things differently. These regrets can weigh heavily on your heart, making the grieving process even more challenging. Adjusting to new family dynamics can also be emotionally taxing. The relationships within your family may change as everyone navigates their own grief. You might feel isolated if your family members grieve in ways that are different from your own. Acknowledging these feelings and understanding that they are a natural part of the grieving process is important.

Coping with the loss of a parent requires finding ways to honor their memory while managing your own grief. Creating new traditions can be a meaningful way to keep their memory alive. For example, you might choose to celebrate their birthday each year by doing something they loved, such as cooking their favorite meal or visiting a place that was special to them. These new traditions can provide comfort and a sense of connection to your parent. Seeking therapy or counseling can also be incredibly beneficial. A professional can help you navigate the complex emotions and challenges that come with losing a parent. They can provide strategies for coping and offer a safe space to express your feelings.

I remember a woman who lost her mother unexpectedly. She shared how she struggled with feelings of regret and guilt, wishing she had spent more time with her. She started a scholarship fund in her name to honor her mother's memory, helping students pursue their education. "It was a way to turn my grief into something positive," she said. Another person I spoke with, who lost his father, found solace in counseling. "Talking to a therapist helped me process my emotions and find a way to move forward," he explained. He also joined a support group for adults who had lost parents, which provided a sense of community and understanding.

These personal stories highlight the diverse ways individuals cope with the loss of a parent. Each person's journey is unique, and there is no right or wrong way to grieve. Finding what works for you is key. Whether it's creating new traditions, seeking professional help, or connecting with others who have experienced a similar loss, there are many paths to healing. Remember, it's okay to seek support and take the time you need to process your grief. The loss of a parent is a profound experience, and it's important to be gentle with yourself as you navigate this difficult time.

In the face of such a significant loss, it's crucial to find ways to honor your parents' memory and take care of your own emotional well-being. Creating new traditions, seeking therapy, and connecting with others can provide the support and comfort you need. Grief is a deeply personal experience, and finding the right path for you is important.

GRIEF AFTER LOSING A SIBLING

Losing a sibling is a unique kind of heartbreak. Unlike the loss of a parent, spouse, or child, a sibling's death often means losing a piece of your own identity. Your sibling is someone who shares your history, your memories, and your experiences. They often understand your family dynamics the best, know your childhood secrets, and have been a constant presence in your life. It feels like a part of your past is lost with them when they are gone. This loss can bring about a profound sense of isolation as you realize that no one else can fully understand the bond you shared.

The death of a sibling also changes the family dynamics in profound ways. You might find yourself taking on new roles within the family, such as becoming the primary source of support for your parents or other siblings. The absence of your sibling may shift the balance within the family, leading to new responsibilities and expectations. This can be overwhelming, especially as you are dealing with your own grief. The changes in family roles can also lead to tension and conflict as each family member navigates their own grief journey in different ways.

Emotionally, losing a sibling can bring a complex mix of feelings. You might experience survivors' guilt, questioning why you are still here while they are not. This guilt can be a heavy burden, leading to feelings of unworthiness or self-blame. Anger is another common emotion directed at yourself, your sibling, or even the situation that took them away. This anger can be confusing and difficult to process, as it often coexists with profound sadness. The grief you feel for your sibling is multifaceted, combining the pain of losing a loved one with the loss of a shared history and future.

Coping with the loss of a sibling requires finding ways to honor their memory and support your healing. Joining sibling support groups can be incredibly helpful. In these groups, you can connect with others who have experienced similar losses, share your stories, and find comfort in their understanding. Support groups provide a safe space to express your emotions and receive validation from those who truly get it. Creating memorials to honor your sibling is another way to cope. This could be as simple as a photo album or as significant as a dedicated event or scholarship in their name. These acts of remembrance help keep their memory alive and provide a sense of purpose in your grief.

One person I met, Sarah, lost her older brother to a sudden illness. She found solace in joining a sibling support group, where she could talk about her brother and listen to others share their stories. "It was a place where I could be honest about my pain," she said. "Hearing others talk about their siblings made me feel less alone." Sarah also created a memorial garden in her backyard, planting her brother's favorite flowers. "Tending to the garden gives me a way to feel connected to him," she explained. Another individual, Michael, lost his sister in a tragic accident. He found comfort in writing letters to her, which he kept in a special box. "Writing to her helps me process my emotions," he shared. "It's like I'm keeping our conversation going."

These real-life stories highlight the importance of finding personal ways to cope with sibling loss. Whether through support groups, memorials, or personal rituals, there are many paths to healing. It's important to find what works for you and remember there is no right or wrong way to grieve. Seeking support and finding meaningful ways to honor your sibling can help you navigate this difficult time.

Support groups specifically for siblings can be invaluable resources. Here are some that may be helpful:

Support Groups for Siblings Who Have Lost a Sibling

- **The Compassionate Friends**: Offers support groups for siblings nationwide and online resources.
- **Sibling Support Project**: Provides support and resources for siblings dealing with the loss of a brother or sister.
- **Sibling Grief**: An online community where siblings can share their stories and find support.

Losing a sibling is a profound and unique loss, but you don't have to navigate it alone. Reaching out for support and finding ways to honor your sibling's memory can provide comfort and help you find a path forward. Remember, it's okay to seek help and take the time you need to heal.

CHAPTER 2
NAVIGATING DAILY LIFE AMID GRIEF

I remember the first morning after Brittney's sudden passing. The world felt both too fast and too slow, and even the simplest tasks seemed insurmountable. I stood in the kitchen, staring at the clock, feeling a deep sense of disorientation. The routine of making coffee, something I had done countless times, felt foreign and overwhelming. In these moments of daily life, grief shows its relentless nature, affecting every aspect of our existence. This chapter is about managing these daily responsibilities while allowing yourself the space to grieve.

COPING WITH DAILY RESPONSIBILITIES

Even the smallest tasks can feel like monumental challenges when you're grieving. Prioritizing your tasks and setting realistic goals can be a lifesaver. Start by breaking down your day into manageable chunks. Using a planner or a calendar can help you visualize your day and keep track of essential tasks. Write down what you must do, but keep your list short and achievable. Focus on the essentials and let go of the non-essential tasks for now. It's okay to simplify your life during this time. For instance, opt for simple, nutritious options that require minimal effort instead of cooking elaborate meals.

Delegating responsibilities is another crucial step in managing your daily life while grieving. It's important to recognize that you don't have to do everything yourself. Reach out to friends, family, or colleagues and ask for their help. This can be incredibly difficult if you're used to being self-reliant, but it's a necessary part of healing. Tasks like grocery shopping, household chores, or even managing paperwork can be delegated. Clear communication is key. Let your support system know exactly what you need. You might say, "I'm finding it difficult to keep up with house cleaning. Would you mind helping me with that this week?" Most people are willing to help; they just need to know how.

Establishing a routine can provide a sense of normalcy and stability amid the chaos of grief. Start with small, manageable routines. Create a morning routine that includes simple activities like making your bed, having a cup of tea, or going for a short walk. Similarly, an evening routine can help signal to your body that it's time to wind down. This could include activities like reading a book, taking a warm bath, or practicing some gentle stretches. Scheduling breaks and self-care activities throughout the day are equally important. These can be moments to pause, breathe, and check in, ensuring you're not pushing yourself too hard.

Technology can be an invaluable tool in managing daily responsibilities during this time. Task management apps like

Todoist or Trello can help you keep track of your to-do list and set reminders for important tasks. These apps allow you to break tasks into smaller steps, making them more manageable. You can prioritize tasks by their importance and set deadlines to keep yourself on track. Additionally, reminder apps can help you remember important dates and appointments, preventing them from slipping through the cracks. These tools can reduce the cognitive load, allowing you to focus more on your healing process.

During grief, it's important to be kind to yourself and recognize that it's okay to ask for help and simplify your life. Prioritizing tasks, delegating responsibilities, establishing routines, and using technology to stay organized can make daily life more manageable. These strategies are not about ignoring your grief but creating a supportive framework that allows you to navigate your emotions while maintaining some semblance of normalcy. Remember, it's okay to take things one step at a time and to seek support when you need it.

PRACTICAL TIPS FOR BALANCING WORK AND GRIEF

Balancing work and grief can seem impossible, but open communication with your employer can make a significant difference. It's crucial to share your situation and seek understanding and flexibility. Start by requesting a meeting with your supervisor to discuss your current circumstances. Be honest about your needs and limitations. You might request flexible hours or the possibility of working remotely if your job allows it. Explain how these adjustments can help you maintain your productivity while managing your grief. If necessary, discuss the option of taking temporary leave. Many companies offer bereavement leave; some might even provide additional time off under certain circumstances. Being upfront and clear about your needs can foster a supportive work environment.

Setting boundaries at work is another essential step in protecting your mental health while fulfilling your job responsibilities. It's important to manage your workload and set realistic expectations for yourself and your employer. Communicate with your team about your current capacity and prioritize tasks that are most critical. Setting limits on your working hours can prevent burnout. Make it clear that you need to leave work at a specific time each day to focus on your personal well-being. This might mean saying no to extra projects or delegating tasks to colleagues. Protecting your mental space is vital during this time, and setting boundaries can help you achieve a healthier work-life balance.

Utilize workplace resources available to support you during your grief. Many companies offer Employee Assistance Programs (EAPs), which provide counseling services and support groups. These resources can be invaluable in helping you navigate your emotions and find strategies to cope. Contact your HR department to learn about the specific programs and services your workplace offers. Joining a support group through your EAP can connect you with others who understand your experience, providing a sense of community and shared understanding. Counseling services can offer professional guidance and tools to help you manage your grief while maintaining your work responsibilities.

Implementing stress management techniques in the workplace can significantly impact your ability to cope with grief. Simple practices such as breathing exercises can help reduce stress and anxiety. Take a few moments throughout the day to practice deep, mindful breathing. This can help center your thoughts and provide a brief respite from overwhelming emotions. Taking short breaks during the workday is also essential. Step away from your desk, go for a walk, or find a quiet place to relax. These breaks can help you recharge and maintain focus. Creating a calming workspace can also make a difference. Personalize your workspace with items that bring you comfort, such as photos, plants, or meaningful objects. A calming environment can provide a sense of peace amid the chaos of grief.

Incorporating these practical tips can help you find a balance between work and grief. Open communication with your employer, setting boundaries, utilizing workplace resources, and implementing stress management techniques are all steps that can make a significant difference in your daily life. Remember, it's okay to seek help and take the time you need to care for yourself.

SLEEP AND CONCENTRATION: OVERCOMING COMMON CHALLENGES

Grief can wreak havoc on your sleep patterns, leaving you feeling exhausted and unable to face the day. Insomnia is a common issue, where you lie awake for hours, your mind racing with thoughts and memories. It's as if your brain refuses to shut down, replaying moments over and over.

Nightmares or night sweats can also disrupt your rest, jolting you awake with a pounding heart and a sense of dread. These disturbances make it difficult to get the restorative sleep you need to cope with your emotions and daily responsibilities.

Creating a sleep-friendly environment is crucial for combating these issues. Start by ensuring your bedroom is cool and dark; a lower temperature can help signal to your body that it's time to sleep. You might use blackout curtains to block out light and maintain a consistent sleep schedule. White noise machines or earplugs can drown out disruptive sounds, creating a more peaceful atmosphere. Avoid screens at least an hour before bedtime; the blue light emitted by phones and computers can interfere with your body's natural sleep-wake cycle. Instead, opt for activities that help you wind down, like reading a calming book or practicing gentle stretches.

Concentration can also be a significant challenge when you're grieving. It's easy to feel scattered, your thoughts flitting from one thing to another without settling. Time-blocking techniques can help manage this. You create a structure that can guide you through your day by dedicating specific blocks of time to different tasks. For example, you might set aside an hour in the morning for work tasks, followed by a short break, and then another block for personal errands. Using apps like Focus@Will, which offers background music designed to improve concentration, can also be beneficial. These tools help create an environment conducive to focus, allowing you to accomplish tasks more efficiently.

Incorporating relaxation techniques before bed can significantly improve your sleep quality. Guided meditation or mindfulness exercises can help calm your mind and prepare your body for rest. Plenty of apps and online resources offer guided meditations specifically designed for sleep. These practices encourage you to focus on your breath and let go of the day's stresses. Reading a calming book can also be a soothing pre-sleep ritual. Choose something light and uplifting, avoiding anything too stimulating or emotionally heavy. These activities signal to your mind that it's time to transition from the busyness of the day to the tranquility of sleep.

It's common to struggle with sleep and concentration during grief. These challenges can feel insurmountable, but you can manage them by creating a sleep-friendly environment, implementing time-blocking techniques, and incorporating relaxation practices. It's about finding small, practical steps to help you navigate daily life while honoring your need to grieve.

SELF-CARE STRATEGIES FOR EMOTIONAL WELL-BEING

Practicing self-compassion is crucial When navigating the turbulent waters of grief. It's easy to be hard on yourself during this time, but being kind to yourself can make a significant difference. Start with positive affirmations, which are simple yet powerful statements you can repeat to remind yourself of your worth and resilience. Phrases like "I am doing my best" or "It's okay to feel this way" can help shift your mindset. Journaling can also be a therapeutic way to practice self-compassion. Write about your feelings without judgment. Acknowledge your pain and remind yourself that it's okay to grieve. This exercise can help you process your emotions and offer yourself the kindness you deserve.

Engaging in activities that bring joy is another vital aspect of self-care. While it might seem impossible to find joy amid grief, small moments of happiness can provide much-needed relief. Think about hobbies or activities that you used to enjoy. Whether it's painting, gardening, or playing an instrument, these activities can offer a sense of normalcy and comfort. Spending time with pets can also be incredibly soothing. Animals provide unconditional love and companionship, which can be a great source of comfort during difficult times. Their presence can help you feel less alone and more connected to the present moment.

Setting time aside for relaxation is essential for recharging your emotional batteries. Grief can be exhausting, and relaxing can help restore your energy. Consider taking warm baths, which can be both physically and emotionally soothing. The warmth of the water can help relax your muscles and calm your mind. Listening to soothing music is another excellent way to unwind. Create a playlist of calming songs or nature sounds that help you feel at peace. These relaxation techniques can create moments of tranquility in your day, providing a break from the intensity of your emotions.

It's also important to recognize when professional help is needed. If your emotional well-being is significantly impacted, seeking the support of a therapist or counselor can be incredibly beneficial. Look for professionals specializing in grief counseling, as they have the expertise to help you navigate your feelings and find coping strategies. Online therapy options can also provide accessible support, especially if you find it challenging to leave your home. Platforms like BetterHelp or Talkspace offer virtual sessions with licensed therapists, allowing you to receive support from the comfort of your own space.

During this challenging time, practicing self-compassion, engaging in joyful activities, setting aside time for relaxation, and seeking professional help when needed are all vital strategies for emotional well-being. These self-care practices can help you navigate your grief with kindness and understanding.

MINDFULNESS TECHNIQUES FOR GRIEF MANAGEMENT

Mindfulness is about being present in the moment, fully engaged with whatever you are doing, feeling, or thinking. It involves a non-judgmental awareness of your thoughts and emotions as they arise. The core principles of mindfulness include focusing on the present, accepting what you feel without trying to change it, and observing your experiences without judgment. Practicing mindfulness can significantly benefit your mental health, especially while navigating grief. It helps you become more aware of your emotional state, which can reduce anxiety and improve your overall well-being. By staying present, you can manage overwhelming emotions more effectively and find moments of peace amidst the turmoil.

If you are new to mindfulness, starting with simple exercises can make the practice more approachable. Breathing exercises are a great way to begin. Find a quiet place to sit or lie and focus on your breath. Inhale deeply through your nose, hold for a moment, and then exhale slowly through your mouth. Repeat this process for a few minutes, paying close attention to the sensation of the breath entering and leaving your body.

Another effective exercise is body scan meditation. Lie down comfortably and close your eyes. Starting from your toes, slowly bring your attention to each body part, moving upwards to your head. Notice any sensations, tension, or discomfort and acknowledge them without trying to change anything. This practice helps you connect with your body and can provide a sense of grounding and relaxation.

Incorporating mindfulness into your daily activities can make the practice more sustainable and impactful. Mindful eating is one way to do this. When you eat, focus entirely on the experience. Notice the colors, textures, and flavors of your food. Chew slowly and savor each bite, paying attention to how it feels in your mouth. This practice can turn a routine activity into a moment of mindfulness, grounding you in the present. Mindful walking is another simple yet effective technique. As you walk, pay attention to the sensations in your feet and legs, the rhythm of your steps, and the surrounding environment. Whether you are in a park or walking to your car, this practice can help you stay present and calm. Even household chores can become opportunities for mindfulness. Whether you are washing dishes or folding laundry, focus on the task at hand. Notice the sensations, smells, and sounds involved in the activity. This can transform mundane tasks into moments of mindfulness, providing a break from the constant barrage of thoughts and emotions.

Numerous resources are available for those who want to deepen their mindfulness practice. Books like "The Miracle of Mindfulness" by Thich Nhat Hanh or "Wherever You Go, There You Are" by Jon Kabat-Zinn offer valuable insights and practical advice. Apps like Headspace and Calm provide guided meditations and mindfulness exercises that you can practice anytime, anywhere. Additionally, local mindfulness classes or workshops can offer a community and structured guidance to help you develop your practice further. These resources can provide the support and knowledge needed to make mindfulness a regular part of your life, helping you navigate grief with greater resilience and calm.

NUTRITION AND PHYSICAL EXERCISE TO SUPPORT HEALING

In the depths of grief, taking care of your body might seem like an insurmountable task. However, maintaining a balanced diet can significantly support your emotional and physical health during this difficult time. Nutrient-rich foods play a crucial role in brain health, helping to stabilize mood and energy levels. Foods rich in omega-3 fatty acids like salmon, walnuts, and flaxseeds can help reduce inflammation and support brain function. Leafy greens, berries, and whole grains provide essential vitamins and antioxidants that combat stress and fatigue. Hydration is equally important; drinking enough water helps maintain cognitive function and keeps your body operating smoothly. Even mild dehydration can amplify feelings of tiredness and irritability, so aim to drink water regularly throughout the day.

Meal planning might feel overwhelming, but simple strategies can make it manageable. Start by creating a weekly meal plan. This doesn't have to be elaborate; focus on easy, healthy meals that you can prepare quickly. For instance, batch-cooking a pot of vegetable soup or a tray of roasted vegetables can provide nutritious options for several days. Incorporate a mix of protein, healthy fats, and complex carbohydrates to stabilize your energy levels. Smoothies can be a quick, nourishing option, especially when you don't feel like eating a full meal. Blend fruits, greens, and a protein source like yogurt or a plant-based protein powder for a balanced, nutrient-packed drink.

Physical exercise is another powerful tool in grief recovery. When you're grieving, finding the motivation to move might be challenging, but even gentle exercise can make a significant difference. Physical activity releases endorphins, the body's natural mood lifters, which can help reduce stress and anxiety. Regular exercise can also improve sleep quality, which is often disrupted by grief. Simple activities like walking or jogging in nature can be particularly soothing. The fresh air and change of scenery can provide a mental break from your thoughts and offer a sense of peace. If you prefer a more structured environment, joining a local gym or fitness class can provide both physical benefits and a sense of community.

For those days when intense exercise feels too daunting, gentle options like yoga or tai chi can be incredibly beneficial. These practices improve physical strength and flexibility and promote relaxation and mindfulness. Yoga poses that focus on stretching and breathing can help release physical tension and calm the mind. With its slow, deliberate movements, Tai chi can be a meditative practice that enhances physical and emotional balance. Incorporating light strength training or simple stretching exercises into your daily routine can also help maintain muscle tone and reduce stress.

Remember, the goal is not to push yourself but to find nurturing activities. It's about listening to your body and giving it what it needs. Sometimes, that might be a brisk walk; other times, it might be a gentle stretch or simply sitting quietly and breathing deeply. By prioritizing balanced nutrition and incorporating physical exercise into your routine, you can support your body and mind during this challenging time. These small steps can help you build resilience and find moments of peace amid the storm of grief.

Taking care of your physical health through balanced nutrition and regular exercise is vital to navigating daily life amid grief. While it may seem difficult, these practices can support your body and mind in healing. They offer structure, release, and a way to channel your emotions constructively. As you move forward, remember that it's okay to take small steps, to ask for help, and to be gentle with yourself. This chapter has provided tools to support your physical and emotional well-being, leading us to explore more healing aspects in the next chapter.

CHAPTER 3
COPING MECHANISMS AND EMOTIONAL SUPPORT

One evening, while going through my phone, I stumbled upon a picture of Brittney and me laughing at the beach. The memory hit me like a tidal wave, and I felt overwhelmed with emotion. At that moment, I grabbed a notebook and began to write. I poured my feelings, memories, and sorrow onto the pages. That night, I discovered the profound impact that journaling can have during grief. Writing became a lifeline, a way to process the chaos inside my mind and heart.

JOURNALING PROMPTS FOR EMOTIONAL EXPRESSION

Journaling can be a powerful tool for processing emotions and finding clarity amid the confusion of grief. It offers a safe space to express feelings that might be too difficult to share with others. According to Psychology Today, journaling can relieve stress and provide long-term physical benefits, such as improved immune system functioning and better sleep. Emotionally, it can foster a sense of well-being and reduce symptoms of depression and anxiety. The act of writing allows you to confront distressing thoughts and feelings, leading to emotional release and, ultimately, healing.

One of the most significant benefits of journaling is its emotional release. When you write about your feelings, you give them a voice. This can be incredibly cathartic, helping to lessen your emotional burden. Tracking your progress over time is another benefit. Looking back on your journal entries, you can see how your emotions evolve, which can be reassuring. It shows that while grief is a long process, there is movement and change, even if it's gradual. Journaling also helps you identify patterns in your emotions, which can be insightful for understanding your grief.

To help you get started, here are some specific journaling prompts that encourage deep reflection and emotional expression. One effective prompt is to "write a letter to your loved one." This can be a way to say things you didn't get to say, share your current life with them, or express your love and longing. Another prompt is to "describe a happy memory you shared." This exercise helps you focus on positive moments and keeps the memory of your loved one alive in a joyful way. A third prompt is to ask yourself, "What emotions are you feeling today and why?" This encourages you to explore your feelings and understand their roots, which can lead to greater emotional clarity.

Incorporating guided journaling exercises can provide structure and make the process less daunting. One such exercise is creating a gratitude list. Each day, write down a few things you are grateful for. This practice shifts your focus from what you have lost to what you still have, which can be incredibly uplifting. Another exercise is reflecting on personal growth since the loss. Consider how you have changed, what you have learned, and how you have managed to keep going. This can help you recognize your resilience and strength, even in the face of immense pain.

To illustrate the power of journaling, here are some sample journal entries from individuals who have found it helpful. One person wrote, "Dear Mom, I planted your favorite flowers in the garden today. It felt like a way to connect with you, to bring a piece of you back into my life." Another entry reads, "I remember that summer day at the beach, how we laughed until our sides hurt. Those moments of pure joy are what I hold onto now." A third entry reflects on daily emotions: "Today, I felt a deep sadness in the morning, but writing about it helped. By the afternoon, I noticed a shift, a small glimmer of peace."

Journaling can be a simple yet profound way to navigate the complexities of grief. It offers a space for emotional release, helps track your progress, and provides a canvas for exploring your feelings. You can find clarity and comfort in your writing using specific prompts and guided exercises. Whether you write a little or a lot, putting pen to paper can be a powerful step toward healing.

DEALING WITH UNEXPECTED TRIGGERS

Grief triggers can appear when you least expect them, often catching you off guard and bringing a flood of emotions. These triggers can be anything that reminds you of your loved one. Specific dates or anniversaries, like their birthday or the day they passed away, can be particularly hard. Songs that you both enjoyed, smells that remind you of them, or places you visited together can also bring back memories and feelings that you thought you had managed. Even a simple walk in your neighborhood can become an emotional rollercoaster if you pass by a place with significant memories.

Managing these unexpected triggers requires a set of practical strategies. Deep breathing exercises can be incredibly helpful in these moments. When you feel a wave of grief coming on, find a quiet place, close your eyes, and take slow, deep breaths. Inhale deeply through your nose, hold for a moment, and then exhale slowly through your mouth. Repeat this process until you feel a bit more grounded. Grounding techniques can also be effective. One simple method is the 5-4-3-2-1 exercise. Name five things you can see, four things you can touch, three things you can hear, two things you can smell, and one thing you can taste. This exercise helps shift your focus from your emotional turmoil to your immediate surroundings, bringing a sense of calm.

Creating a safe space at home where you can retreat when triggers become overwhelming can also be beneficial. This space doesn't have to be elaborate; a corner of a room with a comfortable chair, some soft lighting, and meaningful objects like photos or mementos can provide a sanctuary where you can process your emotions in peace. This space can become your go-to spot whenever you need a break from the intensity of your feelings.

Knowing your triggers and how they impact your emotions is crucial for managing them effectively. Keeping a trigger journal can be a powerful tool for this. Each time you encounter a trigger, note down what it was, how it made you feel, and how you responded. Over time, you'll start to see patterns that can help you anticipate and prepare for these moments. Recognizing the early signs of emotional distress, such as tightening in your chest or a sudden rush of sadness, can also enable you to take proactive steps to manage your feelings before they become overwhelming.

Real-life examples can offer valuable insights into how others have managed their grief triggers. One individual, Alex, shared how certain songs would bring him to tears because they reminded him of his late brother. "Every time I heard our favorite band, I felt like I was drowning in memories," he said. To cope, he started using deep breathing exercises whenever he felt the first notes of those songs, and over time, he found that the songs became less overwhelming. Another person, Maria, found that visiting her favorite park, where she used to go with her mother, was unbearable. She created a small memorial garden in her backyard where she could feel close to her mother without the intense memories of the park. "It gave me a way to honor her while also creating a new, safe space for myself," Maria explained. These personal stories highlight the importance of finding individualized strategies that work for you.

MANAGING SIGNIFICANT DATES AND ANNIVERSARIES

Significant dates, such as birthdays, anniversaries, and holidays, can be particularly challenging when you're grieving. These dates are poignant reminders of your loved one, making the absence feel even more profound. Birthdays, which were once joyous occasions, can now feel like painful milestones. Whether of their passing or your wedding, anniversaries bring back memories that can be both beautiful and heartbreaking. Holidays, filled with traditions and family gatherings, can feel incomplete without their presence. Milestones and special occasions, like graduations or family reunions, highlight the gap left by their absence. These moments can trigger intense waves of sadness and longing, which is normal and valid.

Planning ahead can be immensely helpful in navigating these emotionally charged dates. Start by acknowledging that these days will be difficult and permit yourself to feel whatever comes up. Consider creating new traditions that honor your loved one while also allowing you to cope. For instance, if celebrating their birthday feels too painful, you might spend the day doing something they loved, like hiking or visiting a favorite café. Involving friends and family in commemorative activities can also provide comfort and support. Sharing memories, cooking their favorite meal, or simply gathering to talk about them can make the day feel less isolating.

Honoring your loved one on these significant dates can take many forms. Lighting a candle in their memory can be a simple yet powerful act, creating a moment of reflection and connection. Visiting a place that was special to them can provide a sense of closeness and nostalgia. This could be a favorite park, a beach, or even a restaurant where you shared many meals. Donating to a charity in their honor can also be a meaningful way to remember them. Choose a cause they cared about and make a contribution in their name. This act not only honors their memory but also positively impacts their absence.

Personal stories often illuminate the profound ways people cope with these significant dates. I recall a woman named Laura who lost her husband just before their 10th wedding anniversary. She found solace in creating a new tradition of visiting their favorite beach on that day. "We used to walk here every summer," she told me. "Now, I go alone, but I feel him with me in the waves and the wind." Another person, James, shared how he and his siblings gather each year on their mother's birthday to cook her favorite dishes and share stories. "It's like she's still part of our family dinners," he said. "We laugh, we cry, but most importantly, we remember."

Planning ahead, creating new traditions, and involving loved ones can provide structure and support on these difficult days. Each person's way of honoring their loved one is unique, reflecting the individuality of their relationship and the depth of their grief. These acts of remembrance not only keep the memory of your loved one alive, but also offer moments of connection and healing.

CREATING A SUPPORT NETWORK

When my world turned upside down, one of the most crucial elements that helped me cope was having a solid support network. During the grieving process, a support network provides not only emotional support but also practical assistance. The emotional support is invaluable; it's the shoulder to cry on, the listening ear, the comforting presence that reassures you that you are not alone in your sorrow. Knowing that someone is there to share your burden can make the weight of grief more bearable. Practical assistance comes in various forms, from helping with daily chores to managing overwhelming tasks. Simple acts like cooking a meal, running errands, or accompanying you to appointments can make a significant difference.

Identifying potential members for your support network is the next step. Family members are often the first people you turn to. They are likely to be experiencing the same loss and can offer mutual support. Friends, especially those who have been through similar experiences, can provide a different understanding and comfort. They may offer perspectives and coping strategies that you might not have considered. Support groups or online communities are also valuable resources. These groups consist of individuals who are going through similar experiences, and they provide a safe space to share your feelings and find solace in knowing that others understand your pain.

Building and maintaining a strong support network requires clear communication and setting boundaries. Start by communicating your needs honestly. Let your network know what kind of support you need, whether it's emotional or practical. Be specific; instead of saying, "I need help," you might say, "Can you help me with grocery shopping this week?" Setting boundaries is equally important. Grieving is an intensely personal process, and there may be times when you need space. It's okay to let your network know when you need time alone. Seeking out support groups or counseling services can also be beneficial. These resources provide professional guidance and a structured environment where you can explore your feelings without judgment.

I remember Jane, who found herself struggling after the sudden loss of her partner. She felt isolated and overwhelmed by the responsibilities that fell solely on her shoulders. She gradually built a network of support by reaching out to her siblings and close friends. Her sister started helping with household chores, while her best friend checked in daily, providing a listening ear. Jane also joined an online support group for individuals who had lost their partners. "It was a game-changer," she said. "Knowing that others understood my pain made me feel less alone." Jane's story highlights the importance of having a diverse support network that caters to different aspects of your needs.

Building a support network is not just about asking for help; it's also about allowing yourself to receive it. Many people find it difficult to accept help, feeling they should be strong and self-reliant. However, opening up to support can be incredibly healing. Accepting help doesn't make you weak; it makes you human. It's a step toward healing and finding your way through the darkness of grief. Remember, your support network is there to help lighten your load, not to judge you. Let them in, allow them to support you, and in doing so, you will find the strength to keep moving forward, one step at a time.

Consider the story of Mark, who lost his mother unexpectedly. He initially resisted leaning on others, feeling he needed to be strong for his family. However, the burden became too much to bear alone. He eventually reached out to his church community and found a group of compassionate individuals ready to support him. One member, an older woman who had lost her son years before, became his mentor. "She taught me that it's okay to lean on others," Mark said. "Her wisdom and support were my lifeline." Mark's experience underscores the profound impact a well-rounded support network can have during grief.

VALIDATION AND NORMALIZATION OF EMOTIONS

When I lost someone close to me, I often found myself swimming in a sea of unspoken emotions. Each wave of sadness, anger, or guilt felt isolating as if I were the only one experiencing such depth of grief. It wasn't until I started to validate these feelings that I began to find some semblance of peace. Emotional validation is crucial during times of grief. It reduces feelings of isolation by affirming that what you're experiencing is real and legitimate. When you acknowledge your emotions, it enhances your emotional resilience. Instead of bottling up your feelings, you give them space to feel and process, which can be incredibly healing.

There are several techniques for self-validation that can help you navigate your grief. Affirmation exercises are a simple yet effective way to start. Every morning or evening, take a moment to speak kindly to yourself. Phrases like, "It's okay to feel this way," or "My emotions are valid," can shift your mindset and provide comfort. Reflective journaling is another powerful tool. Spend a few minutes each day writing about your emotions. Don't worry about grammar or structure; just let your thoughts flow. This practice allows you to see your emotions on paper, making them tangible and easier to understand. Writing can also help you track your emotional journey, offering insights into how your feelings evolve over time.

Seeking external validation is equally important. Talking to trusted friends or family members can provide a different kind of support. These conversations don't have to be elaborate. Sometimes, just saying, "I'm really struggling today," can open the door to meaningful dialogue. Your loved ones can offer perspectives and reassurance that you might be unable to give yourself. Joining support groups is another excellent way to receive external validation. In these groups, you'll find individuals going through similar experiences. Sharing your story and hearing others share theirs can create a sense of community and mutual understanding. These groups provide a safe space to express your feelings without fear of judgment.

I remember one story vividly. A woman named Lisa lost her father unexpectedly. She felt overwhelmed by guilt and sadness, believing she should have done more. One day, she confided in her best friend about her feelings. Her friend listened without interrupting, simply affirming Lisa's emotions. "It's natural to feel this way," her friend said. "Your love for your dad is evident in your grief." That simple act of validation was a turning point for Lisa. She realized she wasn't alone in her feelings and sought additional support. Lisa also joined a local support group where she found others who had lost parents. Sharing her story and hearing others helped her feel understood and less isolated.

Another person, Tom, found validation through his therapist. Tom struggled with anger after his brother's sudden death. He felt guilty for being angry and worried that it made him a bad person. In therapy, his counselor helped him see that anger is a natural part of grief. "Anger is an expression of your pain," his counselor explained. "It's okay to feel it." This validation allowed Tom to explore his anger without judgment, leading to a deeper understanding of his emotions. He also started using affirmation exercises, telling himself, "My feelings are valid," whenever the anger resurfaced. Over time, Tom found that acknowledging his emotions reduced their intensity and helped him cope more effectively.

Internal and external validation plays a vital role in the grieving process. It helps you recognize that your emotions are a natural response to loss, reducing feelings of isolation and enhancing emotional resilience. Techniques like affirmation exercises and reflective journaling can provide self-validation while seeking support from friends, family, and support groups offers external validation. Personal stories, like Lisa and Tom's, highlight the transformative power of feeling understood and accepted. By validating your emotions, you allow yourself to grieve openly and authentically, paving the way for healing and growth.

PRACTICAL EXERCISES FOR DAILY COPING

Daily coping exercises can provide a lifeline when you're navigating the storm of grief. These exercises, which include routine-building and emotional regulation techniques, offer practical ways to manage your grief daily. Establishing routines can create a sense of normalcy and predictability in a time when everything feels chaotic. Emotional regulation techniques help you manage the intense feelings of loss, allowing you to find moments of peace amid the turmoil.

Various coping exercises can be integrated into your daily life to help manage grief. Breathing exercises for stress relief are simple yet effective. Find a quiet place to sit or lie down comfortably. Close your eyes and take a deep breath in through your nose, filling your lungs completely. Hold your breath for a moment, then slowly exhale through your mouth. Repeat this process several times, focusing solely on your breath. This can help calm your nervous system and reduce anxiety. Grounding techniques are also useful for staying present. As mentioned before, an effective method is the 5-4-3-2-1 technique: identify five things you can see, four things you can touch, three things you can hear, two things you can smell, and one thing you can taste. This exercise helps anchor you in the present moment, breaking you from overwhelming emotions. Visualization exercises for emotional balance can also be beneficial. Close your eyes and imagine a peaceful place where you feel safe and calm. Spend a few minutes visualizing the details of this place—the sights, sounds, and smells. This mental escape can provide a sense of tranquility and balance.

To perform deep breathing exercises, follow these step-by-step instructions. First, find a comfortable, quiet space where you won't be disturbed. Sit or lie down and close your eyes. Place one hand on your chest and the other on your abdomen.

Take a slow, deep breath in through your nose, allowing your abdomen to rise as your lungs fill with air. Hold the breath for a few seconds, then slowly exhale through your mouth, feeling your abdomen fall. Repeat this process for five to ten minutes, focusing on the rhythm of your breath. This exercise can help reduce stress and promote relaxation.

For visualization exercises, use this simple script to calm your mind. Begin by finding a quiet, comfortable place to sit or lie down. Close your eyes and take a few deep breaths, allowing your body to relax. Imagine yourself in a peaceful place like a beach, forest, or meadow. Picture the details of this place, the colors, sounds, and scents. Visualize yourself walking through this serene environment, feeling the warmth of the sun or the coolness of the breeze. Spend a few minutes immersing yourself in this visualization, allowing it to bring a sense of calm and balance. When you're ready, slowly bring your attention back to the present moment, carrying the feelings of tranquility.

One individual, Emily, found deep breathing exercises to be a crucial part of her daily routine after losing her sister. "I would wake up feeling overwhelmed but taking a few minutes to breathe deeply helped me start my day a bit calmer," she shared. This practice allowed Emily to manage her anxiety and find moments of peace throughout her day. Another person, John, used grounding techniques to stay present during overwhelming moments. He explained, "Whenever I felt a wave of grief coming on, I would use the 5-4-3-2-1 technique. It helped me focus on the here and now rather than getting lost in my thoughts." This simple exercise provided

John with a tool to manage his emotions and stay connected to the present.

These stories highlight the effectiveness of daily coping exercises in managing grief. By incorporating breathing exercises, grounding techniques, and visualization practices into your daily routine, you can find practical ways to navigate the intense emotions that come with loss. These exercises offer moments of calm, helping you manage your grief one day at a time.

CHAPTER 4
REAL-LIFE STORIES AND TESTIMONIALS

I remember sitting in a quiet café, sipping my coffee, when an elderly man approached me. He was carrying a well-worn book and a gentle smile. He introduced himself as Thomas and asked if he could join me. As we chatted, he began to share the story of his late wife, Margaret, and the profound impact her loss had on his life. His words were filled with both sorrow and resilience, painting a vivid picture of love, loss, and the journey towards finding new purpose. This encounter reminded me of the power of sharing our stories and how they can offer solace and understanding to others who are grieving.

PERSONAL STORIES OF SPOUSAL LOSS

Thomas's journey is a testament to the resilience of the human spirit. Having shared over five decades with Margaret, her passing left him feeling adrift. "I never thought I could live without her," he confessed, "but I find new strength each day." In the initial months, Thomas focused on rebuilding his social life, something Margaret had always encouraged. He joined a local book club, where he found companionship and a shared love for literature. The act of engaging with others helped him combat the loneliness that threatened to overwhelm him. Through these interactions, Thomas discovered a renewed sense of purpose, finding joy in community involvement and the simple pleasure of reading.

Rachel, a young widow in her early thirties, is on the other end of the spectrum. She lost her husband, Daniel, to a sudden heart attack. Rachel's world turned upside down overnight. "We had so many plans, so many dreams," she said, her voice tinged with both sadness and determination. To cope, Rachel threw herself into new hobbies and interests. She took up painting, a passion she had long neglected. "It was like therapy," she explained. "Each stroke of the brush helped me process my emotions." Rachel also found solace in volunteering at a local animal shelter. Caring for the animals provided a sense of purpose and a way to channel her grief into something positive.

In sharing these stories, it's important to recognize that the experience of spousal loss is not confined to any one age or background. Take the story of Alex and Mark, a same-sex couple who had been together for nearly twenty years. When Alex passed away suddenly, Mark was left to navigate a world that often didn't acknowledge the depth of their relationship. "It was like losing a part of myself," he said. Mark found comfort in community involvement, specifically in LGBTQ+ support groups. "I needed to be around people who understood," he shared. These groups provided a space where Mark could express his grief openly and find support from others who had faced similar losses.

Losing a spouse often leads to significant shifts in personal identity. For many, it means adjusting to being single again and redefining personal goals and aspirations. Thomas, for instance, found that his identity had been deeply intertwined with Margaret. "We were always referred to as 'Thomas and Margaret,'" he recalled. "Learning to be just 'Thomas' was a challenge." He began to explore activities and interests that were uniquely his own, discovering a love for gardening that became a new avenue for self-expression. Rachel, too, faced the daunting task of redefining her future. "I had to figure out who I was without Daniel," she said. She set new personal goals, including pursuing further education in art therapy, a field that had become her passion.

These stories highlight the varied experiences of spousal loss and the different ways individuals cope and find new purpose. Each person's journey is unique, shaped by their relationship with their spouse and their personal resilience. The common thread is the strength found in community, new interests, and the courage to redefine one's identity. As Thomas poignantly said, "Her memory guides me in everything I do." These words encapsulate the enduring impact of a loved one and how their memory continues to shape and inspire those left behind.

TESTIMONIES FROM PARENTS WHO LOST A CHILD

When I sat with Maria, a mother who had lost her infant son, the rawness of her grief was palpable. Maria had lost her baby to sudden infant death syndrome (SIDS), an event that left her life shattered. "Holding him for the last time was the hardest moment of my life," she shared, tears streaming down her face. To cope, Maria established a memorial fund in her son's name, which provided resources for other parents facing similar tragedies. "It gave me a sense of purpose," she said. "Helping others felt like a way to honor his short life." Through this act, Maria found a way to channel her grief into something meaningful, creating a legacy for her son that went beyond his brief time on earth.

Rebecca's story is different but equally heart-wrenching. She lost her teenage daughter, Emily, in a car accident. The suddenness of the loss left Rebecca grappling with a whirlwind of emotions. "One day, she was here, and the next, she was gone," Rebecca recalled. To navigate her grief, Rebecca joined a support group for bereaved parents. "Talking to others who had lost children helped me feel less alone," she said. The group became a lifeline, providing a safe space to express her pain and find understanding. Rebecca also turned to creative expression, writing poetry to process her emotions. "Each poem was a piece of my heart," she explained. Through writing, she found a way to articulate the inexpressible, giving voice to her sorrow and her love for Emily.

James, a father who lost his adult son, Michael, to a long battle with illness, shared his journey of coping with the loss. "Watching him suffer and then losing him was the hardest thing I've ever faced," James said. To keep Michael's memory alive, James started a scholarship fund in his son's name, supporting students pursuing careers in healthcare. "Michael always wanted to help others," he explained. "This scholarship is a way to continue his mission." James also found solace in community involvement, participating in local events that raised awareness about the illness that took his son. "Being part of something bigger helped me feel connected to Michael's legacy," he added.

The impact of losing a child extends beyond the parents, affecting the entire family dynamic. Maria shared how her relationship with her spouse and surviving children changed. "We had to learn to communicate openly about our grief," she said. "It wasn't easy, but it brought us closer." Rebecca echoed this sentiment, describing how the loss of Emily brought her family together in unexpected ways. "We leaned on each other," she explained. "We talked about Emily, shared our memories, and supported each other through the hardest days." Open communication became a crucial part of their healing process, allowing each family member to express their grief and feel understood.

James reflected on the importance of strengthening family bonds after losing Michael. "We made a conscious effort to spend more time together," he said. "We took family trips, had regular dinners, and created new traditions." These efforts helped the family navigate their grief, providing moments of joy and connection. "Her laughter still echoes in our home, even in her absence," Rebecca shared, a testament to the enduring presence of her daughter in their lives. James added, "We honor his memory by living fully, as he would have wanted." These reflections highlight the resilience of families navigating the profound loss of a child, finding ways to support each other and keep the memory of their loved ones alive.

SIBLING LOSS: STORIES OF SURVIVAL AND STRENGTH

When I met Jason, he was just a young boy who had lost his older sister to a tragic accident. The pain in his eyes was unmistakable, a reflection of a loss that seemed too vast for someone so young. Jason shared how he struggled to understand why his sister was no longer there to guide him, to share secrets, and to laugh together. "I felt like a part of me was gone," he said softly. To cope, Jason's family helped him create a memory box filled with his sister's favorite items—her stuffed animals, her drawings, and even her perfume. This tangible connection to his sister brought Jason comfort, allowing him to hold onto the beautiful memories they had shared.

For Sarah, losing her brother in adulthood presented a different set of challenges. She described how her brother had always been her rock, the one person she could turn to no matter what. His sudden death left her feeling unmoored, struggling to find her footing in a world without him. To honor his memory, Sarah took up running, an activity her brother had loved. "Each step feels like he's running with me," she explained. Sarah also joined a sibling grief support group, where she found solace in connecting with others who understood her pain. "Sharing our stories made me feel less alone," she said. The group provided a space for Sarah to express her grief and find strength in the collective support.

Navigating the sudden death of a sibling can be particularly harrowing. David, who lost his sister in a car accident, recounted the shock and disbelief that followed. "One moment she was here, and the next, she was gone," he said, his voice filled with sorrow. David found it challenging to process the abruptness of her loss. To cope, he created a small garden in his backyard, planting flowers that his sister loved. "Tending to the garden feels like a way to keep her spirit alive," he shared. David also sought support through online forums dedicated to sibling loss, where he connected with others facing similar heartbreak. "Their stories gave me hope and strength," he added.

Losing a sibling often leads to significant changes in family roles and dynamics. When Jason's sister passed away, he found himself taking on more responsibilities within the family. "I had to grow up faster," he said. This shift brought both challenges and a sense of maturity. For Sarah, the loss of her brother strengthened her bond with her remaining siblings. "We leaned on each other more than ever," she shared. However, not all families experience strengthened bonds. David mentioned how his sister's death initially strained their family relationships. "We all grieved differently, and it caused some tension," he explained. Over time, open communication helped them navigate these changes and find a new sense of unity.

Reflecting on these experiences, it's clear that the loss of a sibling leaves an indelible mark. Jason's words resonate deeply: "I carry her spirit with me in everything I do." This sentiment echoes Sarah's reflection on her brother's enduring presence: "His absence is a void, but his memory is a light that guides me." These quotes capture the profound impact that siblings have on our lives and the ways in which their memory continues to shape and inspire us. Each story underscores the unique and powerful bond between siblings, a bond that transcends even the deepest loss.

LOSING A PARENT: EXPERIENCES AND INSIGHTS

When I met Emily, she was only nine years old and had recently lost her mother to a long battle with cancer. The impact of this loss on her young life was profound and far-reaching. Emily spoke about how her mother's absence created a void that nothing else could fill. "I miss her every day," she said quietly. As Emily grew older, she realized that her mother's wisdom continued to guide her. "Her words still echo in my mind, helping me make decisions," she shared. The long-term impact of losing a parent in childhood often shapes one's emotional landscape, creating a blend of resilience and longing that persists into adulthood.

For Sarah, losing her father at the age of fifty was a different kind of grief. Her father had lived a long and fulfilling life, but his passing still left a significant void. "He was my rock, my advisor," Sarah explained. She found solace in keeping his legacy alive through family traditions as an adult. Every year on his birthday, Sarah and her family would gather to cook his favorite meal and share stories about him. "It's our way of keeping him with us," she said. These traditions provided a sense of continuity and helped Sarah navigate the complexities of grief. Seeking therapy also played a crucial role in her healing process. "Talking to a therapist helped me process my emotions and find a way to move forward," she added.

Jack's experience of losing his mother suddenly was a shock that left him reeling. One day she was there, vibrant and full of life; the next, she was gone. Jack found it incredibly difficult to come to terms with the suddenness of her death. "It felt like the ground had been pulled out from under me," he recalled. To cope, Jack sought support from his community and religious group. Attending weekly meetings and sharing his grief with others who had experienced similar losses provided him with a sense of understanding and connection. "Their support was a lifeline," he said. Engaging in community activities also helped Jack find a new sense of purpose and belonging.

The loss of a parent often leads to significant shifts in family dynamics. For Emily, her mother's death meant stepping into a more mature role within the family. "I had to grow up faster and take on responsibilities I wasn't ready for," she explained. This shift brought both challenges and a sense of resilience. In Sarah's case, losing her father meant becoming the family matriarch, a role she had never anticipated. "I found myself making decisions for the family, something I never thought I'd have to do," she shared. This new role helped strengthen her bond with her surviving family members. "We became closer, supporting each other through the tough times," she added.

Jack's family dynamic also changed significantly after his mother's sudden death. He found that open communication with his siblings and surviving parent was crucial in navigating their shared grief. "We talked openly about our feelings, something we hadn't done much before," he explained. This open communication helped them support each other and find a new sense of unity. "Her wisdom still guides me every day," Jack reflected, highlighting the enduring impact of his mother's teachings. Sarah echoed a similar sentiment, saying, "I honor his memory by living a life he would be proud of." These personal quotes and reflections convey the deep emotional journey of losing a parent and the ways in which their legacy continues to shape and inspire those left behind.

FRIENDSHIPS AND GRIEF: REAL-LIFE ACCOUNTS

When I think of the loss of a childhood friend, I remember the story of Emma and Lily. They had been inseparable since kindergarten, sharing everything from secrets to dreams of the future. One summer, a tragic accident took Lily's life, leaving Emma to navigate a world without her best friend. "Losing Lily felt like losing a part of myself," Emma said, her eyes filled with tears. To cope, Emma created a scrapbook filled with photos, letters, and mementos from their years together. "It's a way to keep her memory alive," she explained. This tangible collection of memories provided Emma with a sense of connection, helping her to process her grief.

The impact of losing a close friend in adulthood can be equally devastating. Mark and Tom have been friends since college, and their bond has grown stronger. When Tom passed away suddenly from a heart attack, Mark was left reeling. "He was my confidant, my brother," Mark shared. To honor Tom's memory, Mark began participating in activities they had loved doing together, like hiking and attending music festivals. "Each hike feels like he's with me," Mark said. He also joined a support group for those grieving friends, finding solace in the shared experiences of others. "Talking to people who understood my pain made a huge difference," he added.

Coping with the sudden death of a friend is often fraught with shock and disbelief. Sarah's friend, Jenny, died in a car accident, leaving Sarah struggling to come to terms with the loss. "One moment she was there, and the next, she was gone," Sarah recalled. To cope, Sarah organized a memorial event where friends and family could share stories and celebrate Jenny's life. "It was a way to come together and remember her," Sarah explained. She also found comfort in creating a keepsake box filled with Jenny's favorite things. "Her laughter is a memory that will never fade," Sarah said, holding a photo of Jenny close.

Losing a friend presents unique challenges that differ from other types of loss. Friends often play a crucial role in our support network, providing companionship and understanding. When a friend passes away, the void they leave can feel insurmountable. Navigating social circles becomes a delicate task, as shared memories with the deceased friend can evoke intense emotions. "Every gathering felt incomplete without him," Mark shared. Finding new ways to engage with social circles and create new memories can be a daunting yet necessary step in the grieving process.

The unique nature of friendship loss also lies in the depth of the bond shared. Friends are the family we choose, and their loss can leave us feeling untethered. Emma reflected on how Lily's death affected her sense of security and belonging. "She was my anchor," Emma said. The absence of a friend who deeply understands us can make us feel isolated. Yet, the memories and the love shared continue to influence and guide us. "His friendship was a gift, and his absence is deeply felt,"

Mark reflected, capturing the enduring impact of his bond with Tom.

Personal reflections and quotes from those who have lost friends highlight the profound emotional journey involved. Sarah's words, "Her laughter is a memory that will never fade," resonate with the enduring presence of her friend Jenny in her life. Mark's sentiment, "His friendship was a gift, and his absence is deeply felt," underscores the irreplaceable nature of a close friend's companionship. These stories and reflections offer a glimpse into the deep and lasting impact that friends have on our lives, even after they are gone.

COMMUNITY SUPPORT: FINDING SOLACE IN SHARED EXPERIENCES

When I first attended a grief support group, I wasn't sure what to expect. The room was filled with people from all walks of life, each carrying their own heavy burden of loss. As we began to share our stories, I realized the profound importance of community support. The shared understanding and empathy in that room were palpable, creating a sense of comfort I hadn't felt since my loved one's passing. It was a reminder that grief, while intensely personal, is also a universal experience. The empathy from others who truly understood my pain provided a level of support that was both comforting and empowering.

In that group, I met Lisa, who had lost her husband suddenly. She described how being surrounded by others who understood her grief became a lifeline. "The support group became my second family during my darkest days," she said. Lisa's experience highlights how community support can build lasting connections through shared grief. These connections are not just fleeting; they often become a crucial part of the healing process. In this space, we could express our feelings without fear of judgment, knowing that everyone else had walked a similar path. It was a sanctuary where our grief was validated, and our emotions were met with compassion.

Community support can take many forms. For some, in-person support groups provide a tangible sense of connection. These groups often meet regularly, allowing members to build trust and rapport over time. In-person meetings offer a structured environment where individuals can share their stories and receive direct support. For others, online forums and social media groups are invaluable. These platforms provide the flexibility to connect with others at any time, offering a sense of community that is always accessible. Online communities can be especially helpful for those who may not have access to local support groups or who prefer the internet's anonymity.

Community events and memorials also play a significant role in providing support. Local events dedicated to remembering loved ones, such as candlelight vigils or memorial walks, offer a way to honor those we have lost while connecting with others who share our pain. These events foster a sense of solidarity, reminding us that we are not alone in our grief. Participating in community memorials can provide a sense of purpose and belonging, helping ease the isolation often accompanying loss.

One woman, Mary, shared how she found support in an online community after losing her son. "I was hesitant at first, but the kindness and understanding I found there were overwhelming," she said. The online forum became a safe space for Mary to express her grief and find comfort in the shared experiences of others. Another individual, John, found solace in a local support group dedicated to those who had lost siblings. "Being surrounded by others who understand has been a lifeline," he shared. These personal reflections underscore the transformative power of community support.

Community support provides a network of empathy and understanding that can be a crucial part of the healing process. The shared experiences and connections formed in these spaces offer comfort and strength, helping individuals navigate their grief with the support of others who truly understand. Whether through in-person groups, online communities, or local events, finding a support community can make a significant difference in the journey through grief. These connections remind us that while our grief is deeply personal, we do not have to face it alone.

MAKE A DIFFERENCE

Unlock the Power of Comfort and Healing

"The best way to find yourself is to lose yourself in the service of others."

MAHATMA GANDHI

Helping others through their hardest times can bring peace and joy into your own life. So, let's make a difference together!

Would you help someone who is struggling with the sudden loss of a loved one? Just like you, they might be searching for answers and a way to heal but not know where to begin.

My goal with *I Didn't Get to Say Goodbye: Healing After the Sudden Death of a Loved One* is to offer comfort, understanding, and practical advice for those going through such a tough time. But to reach more people who need this support, I need your help.

Most people choose books based on reviews. By leaving a review, you could help someone take their first step toward healing after a sudden loss.

It costs nothing and takes only a minute, but your review could make a difference in someone's journey through grief. It could help...

...one more person find hope in their darkest moments.

...one more grieving heart feel understood.

...one more family member heal from the pain of sudden loss.

...one more individual realize they are not alone.

To make a difference, simply scan the QR code below and leave a review:

If you believe in helping others through tough times, you're my kind of person. Thank you from the bottom of my heart!

Jeffrey Simmons

CHAPTER 5
LEGAL AND FINANCIAL GUIDANCE

This is Tom's story, "The day that changed everything is etched in my memory with unwavering clarity. I was sitting in the cold, impersonal space of the hospital waiting room when the doctor approached, his face etched with solemnity. Hearing "I'm sorry for your loss" felt like a shockwave through my system, igniting a blend of disbelief and profound sorrow. In the depth of my grief, I was starkly aware of the immediate need to navigate the legal and financial aftermath of losing someone so suddenly. Understanding the necessary steps became a beacon, offering a glimmer of order and purpose amidst the chaos of loss."

IMMEDIATE STEPS TO TAKE AFTER A LOSS

One of the first things you must do is notify the relevant authorities and individuals about the death. If the death occurs at home, you must contact the local authorities immediately. Dial 911 and inform the dispatcher of the situation. If there is a "Do Not Resuscitate" order, make sure to present it to the paramedics upon their arrival. The police or coroner will issue a legal pronouncement of death, essential for all subsequent steps. If the person passed away in a hospital or under hospice care, the medical staff will handle this for you. Once the authorities are informed, the next step is to notify close family members and friends. This task can be emotionally draining, so consider enlisting the help of a trusted friend or relative to make some of these calls. Informing the deceased's employer is also crucial. Reach out to the HR department to notify them of the death and to discuss any benefits or final paychecks that may be due.

Obtaining the death certificate is a critical step in the legal and financial process. You will need to contact the vital records office in the state where the death occurred. This document is essential for various tasks, from closing bank accounts to claiming life insurance. Requesting multiple copies of the death certificate is advisable, as many institutions require an original certified copy. Most states allow only immediate family members to obtain this document, and you may need proof of your relationship with the deceased. The death certificate will be required to notify the Social Security Administration, close or transfer credit cards, and manage various other legal and financial matters.

Securing the deceased's property is another immediate concern. If they lived alone, you might need to change the locks to prevent unauthorized access. Make sure to gather and safeguard important documents such as the will, insurance policies, account records, and identification documents. These documents are crucial for settling the deceased's affairs. Additionally, ensure that any valuable items are stored securely to prevent theft or loss. If the deceased had pets, plan for their care as well. This ensures that all aspects of the deceased's life are managed responsibly during this transitional period.

Initiating funeral arrangements can feel overwhelming, but taking it step-by-step can make it more manageable. Start by choosing a funeral home. It's helpful to compare a few options to find one that aligns with your needs and budget. Some individuals may have pre-arranged funeral plans, which can simplify the process. If such plans exist, follow the specified instructions. If not, you will need to decide the type of funeral or memorial service, burial or cremation, and any specific wishes the deceased may have had. Communicating with family members about funeral preferences is crucial. This ensures that the service honors the deceased's wishes while also considering the needs and desires of surviving family members. Discussing these preferences openly can help create a service that brings comfort and closure to all involved.

Navigating these immediate steps can feel daunting, but each action you take helps create a sense of order during a chaotic time. Notifying authorities, obtaining the death certificate, securing property, and initiating funeral arrangements are foundational tasks that set the stage for managing the broader legal and financial responsibilities that follow. While each step may bring its own challenges, remember that you don't have to face them alone. Seeking support from friends, family, and professionals can make a significant difference as you navigate this difficult period.

UNDERSTANDING WILLS AND ESTATES

When a loved one passes, understanding the purpose and components of a will becomes crucial. A will is a legal document outlining how a person's assets and affairs should be managed and distributed after death. It essentially serves as a roadmap for handling their estate. The executor of the will is the person appointed to ensure that the deceased's wishes are carried out. This individual manages the estate, pays off debts, and distributes assets to beneficiaries. Beneficiaries are the individuals or organizations named in the will to receive assets, including money, property, or personal items. Specific bequests refer to particular gifts designated for certain beneficiaries, such as a family heirloom left to a grandchild or a sum of money allocated to a charity. Understanding these components helps you see the structure and intent behind a will, providing clarity during a time of loss.

Navigating the probate process is an essential part of managing an estate. Probate is the legal procedure that validates the will and grants the executor the authority to act on behalf of the deceased. It begins with filing the will with the probate court, which formalizes the process. Next, the estate's assets must be inventoried. This means compiling a comprehensive list of all the deceased's property, financial accounts, and personal belongings. The inventory provides a clear picture of the estate's value and helps manage its distribution. Once the assets are accounted for, the executor pays any outstanding debts and taxes. This step ensures that all financial obligations are met before the remaining assets are distributed to the beneficiaries. Understanding these steps can demystify probate and reduce the stress associated with it.

If a person dies without a will, they are said to have died intestate. When this happens, state-specific laws on intestate succession determine how the estate is distributed. These laws vary by state but generally prioritize close family members, such as spouses, children, and parents. The court appoints an administrator to manage the estate, similar to the role of an executor. This administrator is responsible for collecting and managing the assets, paying off debts, and distributing the remaining assets according to state law. The absence of a will can complicate the process, leaving more room for disputes among potential heirs. Understanding intestate succession can help you anticipate and navigate these challenges.

The role of the executor is incredibly important in managing the deceased's estate. This person is entrusted with significant responsibilities, starting with collecting and managing the estate's assets. This involves securing property, accessing financial accounts, and ensuring the safekeeping of valuable items. The executor must also settle debts and liabilities, which means paying off creditors and handling outstanding bills. This step is crucial to ensure that the estate's obligations are met before any assets are distributed. Finally, the executor is responsible for distributing the remaining assets to the beneficiaries as outlined in the will. This process must be handled with care and transparency to honor the deceased's wishes and maintain fairness among the beneficiaries.

When my own family faced the loss of a loved one, the executor played a pivotal role in managing the estate. My

Father was appointed as the executor, and I watched as he meticulously collected assets, handled debts, and ensured that each beneficiary received their designated share. He spent countless hours organizing documents, meeting with lawyers, and communicating with family members to keep everyone informed. His diligence and commitment provided a sense of stability and order during a chaotic time. This experience underscored the importance of the executor's role and the need for clear communication and organization.

Understanding the purpose and components of a will, the probate process, intestate succession, and the responsibilities of the executor can provide clarity and support as you navigate the legal and financial aspects of losing a loved one. Each step, while challenging, is part of honoring their legacy and ensuring that their wishes are respected.

MANAGING DEBTS AND FINANCIAL OBLIGATIONS

When my grandfather passed away suddenly, one of the first challenges my father faced was managing his financial obligations. It's a daunting task, but breaking it down into manageable steps can make it more approachable. The first step is to identify and list all the deceased's debts. Start by gathering financial statements, credit card bills, loan documents, and any other paperwork that might indicate outstanding debts. Look for credit card debts, which are often the most immediate concern. Mortgages and personal loans come next, as these can have significant financial implications. Don't forget about utility bills and subscriptions, which can continue to accumulate charges if not promptly addressed. Compiling a comprehensive list ensures that no debt is overlooked, and it provides a clear picture of the financial landscape you need to navigate.

Notifying creditors of the death is a crucial step in managing these debts. Begin by writing formal notification letters to each creditor. In these letters, include essential information such as the deceased's name, account number, and a brief explanation of the situation. Attach a certified copy of the death certificate to each letter. This document is necessary for creditors to verify the death and update their records accordingly. Addressing these notifications promptly can prevent additional charges and penalties from accruing on accounts. It also opens the door for potential negotiations or settlements, which can be beneficial in managing the overall debt.

Understanding the hierarchy of debt repayment is vital to ensure that the estate is settled fairly and legally. Secured debts should be prioritized first. These debts are backed by collateral, such as a mortgage or car loan. Failure to repay these can result in the loss of the associated property. Once secured debts are addressed, focus on settling unsecured debts, such as credit card balances and personal loans. These debts do not have collateral backing them, but they still need to be paid from the estate's assets. Additionally, consider joint debts and co-signers. If the deceased shared a debt with another person, the surviving co-signer may still be responsible for the remaining balance. Understanding this hierarchy helps you allocate the estate's resources effectively and ensures that all debts are addressed in the proper order.

Negotiating debts with creditors can provide some relief, especially if the estate's assets are limited. Contact creditors directly to discuss the possibility of settlements. Many creditors are willing to negotiate, especially if they understand the financial constraints of the estate. You might be able to settle a debt for less than the full balance, which can free up resources for other obligations. Seeking legal advice can be invaluable in complex situations. An attorney specializing in estate law can provide guidance on the best strategies for negotiating debts and can represent the estate in discussions with creditors. This professional advice can help you navigate legal complexities and ensure that all actions taken are in the estate's best interest.

When Mary's aunt passed away, she was tasked with managing her debts. She started by making a list of all her financial obligations, from credit card debts to her mortgage. Writing the notification letters felt overwhelming at first, but she found a template online that made the process easier. She attached copies of her death certificate and sent them to each creditor. Understanding the hierarchy of debt repayment helped her prioritize her mortgage and car loan first, ensuring no secured property was lost. She was able to negotiate with a few credit card companies, reducing the overall debt burden. Seeking legal advice was a game-changer; the attorney provided clarity and support, helping me navigate the complex landscape of debt management. This experience taught her the importance of organization, clear communication, and professional guidance in managing financial obligations after a loved one's death.

Managing debts and financial obligations after losing a loved one is undoubtedly challenging but taking it step-by-step can make the process more manageable. By identifying and listing all debts, notifying creditors, understanding the hierarchy of debt repayment, and exploring options for negotiating debts, you can ensure that the estate is settled fairly and efficiently. Remember, seeking professional advice can provide additional support and clarity, helping you confidently navigate this difficult task.

NAVIGATING INSURANCE CLAIMS

When someone close passes away, you will find yourself overwhelmed not only with grief but also with the myriad of tasks that need immediate attention. One of the most crucial aspects was navigating insurance claims. Understanding the types of insurance policies that may be relevant after a loved one's death can make this process smoother. Life insurance policies are often the first to come to mind. These policies provide a death benefit to the beneficiaries named in the policy, which can be a crucial financial resource during this difficult time. Health insurance is another important consideration. You will need to notify the health insurance provider to cancel the policy and settle any outstanding medical bills. Homeowner's or renter's insurance also comes into play, especially if the deceased owned property or rented a home. Notifying these providers ensures that the property remains protected and that any claims can be processed.

The next critical step in filing an insurance claim is gathering the necessary documentation. The most important document you will need is the death certificate. As mentioned earlier, obtaining multiple copies of this certificate is advisable, as you will need to submit it to various institutions. Policy documents are also essential. These include the original insurance policy and any related paperwork that outlines the terms and conditions. Contact the insurance company for assistance if you can't locate these documents. Identification and proof of relationship to the deceased are often required as well. This could be a marriage certificate, birth certificate, or any legal document establishing your relationship with the deceased. Having all these documents organized and accessible will streamline the claims process.

Filing the insurance claim involves several steps but breaking it down can make it more manageable. Start by contacting the insurance provider. If the deceased had an insurance agent, they could assist you with the process. If not, reach out to the insurance company directly. Inform them of the death and request the necessary claim forms. Filling out these forms accurately is crucial. Provide all requested information and double-check for any errors, as mistakes can delay the processing of your claim. Once the forms are completed, submit them along with the required documentation. This typically includes the death certificate, policy documents, and proof of relationship. Some insurance companies may allow you to submit these documents online, while others may require physical copies.

Following up on the claim process is essential to ensure timely processing. Keep a detailed record of all communications with the insurance company, including dates, names of representatives you spoke with, and the information discussed. This record can be invaluable if any issues arise. Regularly check the status of your claim to ensure it is progressing. Most insurance companies provide a way to track your claim online or through customer service. If you notice any delays or if additional information is requested, respond promptly to keep the process moving. Persistence and organization can significantly impact how quickly your claim is processed.

When I filed my grandfather's life insurance claim, I found that keeping a detailed record of all communications was incredibly helpful. I maintained a notebook where I logged every phone call, email, and document submission. This kept me organized and provided a clear timeline of the process. I regularly followed up with the insurance company, ensuring my claim was processed. Each time I called, I had my notes ready, which helped me communicate more effectively with the representatives. This attention to detail and persistence paid off, as the claim was processed without unnecessary delays.

Navigating insurance claims after the loss of a loved one can be daunting, but understanding the types of insurance policies, gathering the necessary documentation, filing the claim accurately, and following up diligently can make the process more manageable. Each step you take brings you closer to settling your loved one's affairs and finding a sense of closure amidst the chaos.

LEGAL CONSIDERATIONS FOR SUDDEN DEATH

When faced with sudden death, potential legal issues can arise that need immediate attention. One such issue is the possibility of wrongful death claims. These claims arise when the negligence or misconduct of another party causes someone's death. For example, if a loved one dies in a car accident due to a reckless driver, you may have grounds for a wrongful death lawsuit. This type of claim seeks compensation for the financial and emotional loss experienced by the deceased's family. Wrongful death claims can be complex and emotionally draining, requiring the expertise of a specialized attorney to navigate the legal landscape. Another potential issue is criminal investigations, which may come into play if the death is suspicious or involves foul play. In such cases, law enforcement will investigate whether any criminal activity was involved. This can add another layer of stress and complexity to an already difficult situation.

Consulting with an attorney is crucial when dealing with these legal complexities. Finding a specialized attorney with experience with wrongful death claims or criminal investigations can provide much-needed guidance and support. Start by seeking recommendations from trusted sources or researching online to find attorneys with a proven track record in these areas. Understanding legal fees and costs is also important. Some attorneys work on a contingency basis, meaning they only get paid if you win the case, while others may charge hourly rates or flat fees. Discuss these details upfront to ensure you clearly understand the financial implications. Having a knowledgeable legal representative can help you navigate the intricacies of the legal system and ensure your rights are protected.

Knowing your rights and responsibilities as a family member of the deceased is essential for managing the estate and legal obligations. As a family member, you have rights to the deceased's property and assets, typically outlined in the will. If there is no will, state laws on intestate succession will determine how the assets are distributed. You are also responsible for settling the estate, which includes paying off debts, managing property, and distributing assets to beneficiaries. This process can be overwhelming, especially if you are unfamiliar with estate law. It's important to seek legal advice to ensure you fulfill your responsibilities correctly and protect your rights.

Preparing for potential legal disputes is another important consideration. Family conflicts can arise over the distribution of assets or the interpretation of the will. Mediation and arbitration are effective ways to resolve disputes without going to court. Mediation involves a neutral third party who helps the involved parties reach a mutually agreeable solution. Arbitration, conversely, involves a neutral arbitrator who makes a binding decision on the dispute. These methods can save time, reduce legal costs, and preserve family relationships. However, if disputes cannot be resolved through mediation or arbitration, seeking legal counsel for dispute resolution is necessary. An attorney can provide the expertise and representation needed to navigate court proceedings and ensure a fair outcome.

When a friend's father passed away unexpectedly, the family faced several legal challenges. They suspected medical malpractice and sought the help of a specialized attorney to file a wrongful death claim. The attorney guided them through the process, helping them gather evidence and understand their legal options. The family also faced internal disputes over the distribution of assets, which they initially tried to resolve through mediation. When mediation failed, they had to seek legal counsel to represent them in court. This experience highlighted the importance of having knowledgeable legal representation and understanding the rights and responsibilities of managing an estate.

Addressing potential legal issues, consulting an attorney, knowing your rights and responsibilities, and preparing for potential disputes are all crucial steps in navigating the legal complexities that arise after a sudden death. Each step requires careful consideration and, often, professional guidance to ensure that the deceased's wishes are honored, and the family's rights are protected.

SEEKING PROFESSIONAL FINANCIAL ADVICE

After my grandfather passed away, my dad was suddenly faced with a maze of financial decisions. The emotional toll was heavy enough, but the added stress of managing finances felt overwhelming. During this period, he discovered the immense benefits of seeking professional financial advice. Professional financial advisors can help you navigate complex financial situations that arise after a loved one's death. They can assist in managing immediate financial obligations and guide you through the intricacies of estate planning. Moreover, they can help you plan for future financial stability, ensuring that you make informed decisions that honor your loved one's legacy while securing your own financial future.

Different types of financial professionals offer various kinds of support. Certified Financial Planners (CFPs) are trained to provide comprehensive financial planning. They can help you create a plan that covers everything from managing inheritance to budgeting for future expenses. Estate planning attorneys specialize in the legal aspects of managing and distributing an estate. They can guide you through the probate process, help you understand your rights and responsibilities, and ensure that all legal documents are in order. Tax advisors, on the other hand, can provide specialized knowledge in tax planning and filing. They can help you navigate the complexities of tax obligations that arise after a loved one's death, ensuring that you comply with all legal requirements while minimizing tax liabilities. Each of these professionals brings unique skills to the table, and their combined expertise can provide a holistic approach to managing your financial affairs during this challenging time.

Selecting the right financial advisor is crucial for ensuring that you receive competent and trustworthy guidance. Start by checking their credentials and certifications. For instance, a Certified Financial Planner should have a CFP designation, indicating that they have met rigorous education, examination, and ethical standards. Reviewing and testimonials can also provide insights into the advisor's track record and client satisfaction. Look for feedback that highlights their expertise, communication skills, and reliability. Personal recommendations from friends or family who have had positive experiences can also be valuable. Meeting with potential advisors for an initial consultation can help you assess their approach and compatibility with your needs. During this meeting, ask about their experience with situations similar to yours, their fee structure, and their communication style. Trust your instincts; you should feel comfortable and confident in their ability to guide you.

The scope of financial advice that an advisor can provide is extensive and can cover several critical areas. Managing inheritance and investments is one of the primary areas where they can offer guidance. They can help you understand the best ways to invest any inheritance you receive, ensuring that it aligns with your long-term financial goals. To maximize their potential, they can also advise on managing existing investments, such as stocks, bonds, or real estate. Tax planning and filing are other crucial areas. A financial advisor can help you navigate the tax implications of your inheritance, ensuring that you comply with all regulations while minimizing your tax burden. This includes understanding any estate taxes that may apply and exploring strategies for tax-efficient asset management. Long-term financial planning and budgeting are also essential components of the advice you'll receive. Your advisor can help you create a comprehensive financial plan that accounts for your current needs and future goals. This plan can include budgeting for daily expenses, saving for major life events, and planning for retirement. Your advisor can help you achieve financial stability and peace of mind by providing a clear financial roadmap.

After losing his father, Lincoln turned to a Certified Financial Planner for guidance. The CFP helped him create a detailed financial plan that covered everything from managing his inheritance to planning for future expenses. They provided invaluable advice on investing the funds in a way that aligned with my long-term goals, ensuring that his father's legacy would have a lasting impact. The estate planning attorney he consulted guided him through the probate process, helping him understand his responsibilities and ensuring that all legal documents were in order. The tax advisor also played a crucial role, helping him navigate the complex tax implications of his inheritance and ensuring that he complied with all regulations while minimizing his tax burden. This team of professionals provided comprehensive support, helping him manage the financial aspects of my loss with confidence and clarity.

Seeking professional financial advice after losing a loved one can provide invaluable support and guidance. Financial advisors can help you navigate complex financial situations, plan for future stability, and ensure that you make informed decisions. By selecting the right advisors and understanding the scope of their services, you can manage your financial affairs with confidence and peace of mind. Remember, you don't have to face these challenges alone; professional advisors are there to help you every step of the way.

CHAPTER 6
HELPING CHILDREN COPE WITH GRIEF

I remember the day when Casey, barely five years old, tugged at my sleeve with wide, tear-filled eyes. She asked me, "Why isn't Grandpa coming back?" Her innocent question left me momentarily speechless, grappling for words that could convey the gravity of loss in a way her young mind could understand. At that moment, I realized how crucial it is to help children navigate the tumultuous waters of grief, each age bringing unique challenges and needs.

UNDERSTANDING HOW CHILDREN GRIEVE

Children's understanding of death and their grieving process can vary significantly depending on their age. Infants and toddlers, for instance, sense loss without fully comprehending it. They may not understand the concept of death, but they can feel the absence of a loved one. This often leads to behavioral changes, such as increased clinginess or crying, as they struggle to make sense of the new void in their lives. For toddlers, the world is still a place of concrete experiences, and the absence of a familiar face can cause significant distress.

Preschoolers, on the other hand, often view death as temporary and reversible. They might believe that the deceased person can come back, similar to characters in their favorite cartoons. This stage of development is characterized by magical thinking, where the boundaries between reality and fantasy blur. As a result, preschoolers may ask repeatedly when their loved one is coming back or express beliefs that the person is merely asleep or on a long trip. Their understanding is limited, and their questions might seem repetitive, but they are trying to make sense of a concept that is still beyond their grasp.

School-aged children begin to grasp the finality of death. Around this age, they start to understand that death is permanent and that it happens to everyone eventually. This newfound awareness can lead to increased anxiety, as they may start to worry about the safety of other loved ones or themselves. They might ask more concrete questions about death and what happens afterward. Their grief can manifest in various ways, including academic difficulties, changes in friendships, or physical symptoms like stomachaches and headaches. School-aged children are more capable of expressing their feelings but might still struggle with the complexity of their emotions.

Adolescents understand death similarly to adults, but the emotional turbulence characteristic of this age often intensifies their reactions. They fully grasp the permanence and universality of death, which can lead to existential questions and a deeper sense of loss. Teenagers might experience a wide range of emotions, from profound sadness to anger and even guilt. They might withdraw from family and friends, acting out to cope with their inner turmoil. Adolescents are at a stage where they are forming their own identities, and the loss of a loved one can significantly impact their sense of self and outlook.

Common emotional and behavioral reactions to grief in children can vary widely. Regression in behavior is a typical response, where a child may revert to earlier developmental stages, such as bed-wetting or thumb-sucking. This regression is a coping mechanism for the child to seek comfort and security in familiar behaviors. Changes in sleep and appetite are also common. A grieving child might have trouble falling asleep, experience nightmares, or lose interest in food. Emotional outbursts or withdrawal are other frequent reactions. Children might have sudden episodes of crying, anger, or frustration, or conversely, they might become unusually quiet and detached, retreating into themselves as a way to manage their grief.

A child's previous experiences with loss or trauma can significantly influence their current grief. If a child has previously experienced the death of a family member, they might have a more nuanced understanding of death but also a heightened sensitivity to loss. Changes in family structure, such as divorce, can also impact how a child processes new grief. These past experiences can either provide a framework for understanding and coping or compound their current emotional distress, making it more challenging to navigate their feelings.

Honest communication is crucial in helping children understand and cope with death. It's essential to use clear and age-appropriate language, avoiding euphemisms that can confuse them. Phrases like "passed away" or "gone to sleep" can be misleading. Instead, use straightforward terms like "died" to convey the reality of the situation. This honesty helps children understand what has happened and begins to build a foundation for their grieving process. Children are perceptive and can often sense when something is wrong. Being truthful helps build trust and gives them the clarity they need to start making sense of their loss.

COMMUNICATING ABOUT DEATH WITH CHILDREN

Discussing death with children can feel daunting but using simple and clear language is crucial. When talking to children about death, avoid euphemisms like "gone to sleep" or "passed away," as these can create confusion. Instead, use direct terms like "died" to ensure they understand the permanence of the situation. Answer their questions honestly and directly, even if the answers are difficult. If you don't know the answer, it's okay to admit it. This honesty helps build trust and provides a clearer framework for them to process their grief. Allow children to express their feelings freely. Encourage them to talk about their emotions and listen without judgment. Acknowledge their feelings and let them know feeling sad, angry, or confused is okay.

Keeping the lines of communication open over time is essential. Grief is not a one-time conversation but an ongoing dialogue. Regularly check in with your child about their feelings. Ask open-ended questions like, "How are you feeling today?" or "Is there anything you want to talk about?" Create a safe space where they feel comfortable asking questions and expressing their emotions. Be patient and available for discussions, even if they come at inconvenient times. Grief can resurface unexpectedly, and being there to support your child when they need it can make a significant difference in their healing process.

Using stories and metaphors can be an effective way to help children understand death. Reading books about loss and grief can provide comfort and make the topic more approachable. Stories like "The Invisible String" by Patrice Karst or "When Dinosaurs Die" by Laurie Krasny Brown and Marc Brown offer relatable narratives that can help children make sense of their feelings. Nature metaphors can also be helpful. For example, explaining death as part of the natural cycle, like the changing seasons, can make the concept more tangible. You might say, "Just like the leaves fall from the trees in autumn and new ones grow in spring, life has its own cycles."

Children often have misconceptions about death that need to be addressed. They might think that death is a punishment or that they somehow caused it. Reassure them that death is not a punishment, and explain that it is a natural part of life. Clarify that the child was not at fault for the death. This is especially important if they express feelings of guilt or responsibility. Children might say things like, "If only I had been better," or "Did I do something wrong?" It's crucial to correct these misunderstandings and provide reassurance. Let them know that their loved one died because of reasons beyond anyone's control, and it was not their fault.

Books to Help Children Understand Death and Grief

- **"The Goodbye Book" by Todd Parr**: Explores the range of emotions associated with loss and reassures young readers that things will get better with time.
- **"Wherever You Are My Love Will Find You" by Nancy Tillman**: Offers reassurance to children who have experienced the loss of a parent through the exploration of unconditional love.
- **"I'll Always Love You" by Hans Wilhelm**: Addresses the grief of losing a pet and the comfort of knowing the pet was loved.
- **"The Invisible String" by Patrice Karst**: Comforts children dealing with loss by describing an invisible string that connects people with their loved ones, no matter the separation.
- **"Nana Upstairs & Nana Downstairs" by Tomie dePaola**: Shows love and care for elderly relatives and deals with the death of a great-grandmother and grandmother.
- **"Ida, Always" by Caron Levis**: Explores the emotions felt when a loved one becomes terminally ill and the importance of cherishing the time left.
- **"I Miss You: A First Look at Death" by Pat Thomas**: Introduces concepts like why people die, what a funeral is, and the emotions of saying goodbye in a simple, factual manner.

These books can be a valuable resource in opening up conversations about death and providing comfort to children. By using clear language, maintaining open communication, employing stories and metaphors, and addressing misconceptions, you can help your child navigate the complexities of grief. This supportive approach creates a foundation for healing and resilience during a challenging time.

SUPPORTING A CHILD THROUGH THE GRIEVING PROCESS

One of the most important things you can do for a grieving child is to provide consistent routines and structure. When everything else feels chaotic, maintaining regular meal and bedtime schedules can provide a sense of stability and security. Children find comfort in knowing what to expect next, and routines offer that predictability. Continuing with school and extracurricular activities, as much as possible, can also help. These activities provide a sense of normalcy and offer a distraction from their grief. They also give children an opportunity to interact with peers and engage in physical and creative outlets, which are essential for emotional well-being.

Offering emotional support and validation is crucial. When a child expresses their feelings, acknowledge them without judgment. If they say they're sad, angry, or confused, let them know it's okay to feel that way. Providing physical comfort, like hugs or holding hands, can be incredibly soothing. Simple gestures of affection can communicate love and security when words might fail. Encouraging children to express their emotions through words or creative activities is also vital. Drawing, painting, or writing can offer an outlet for feelings that might be too complex to verbalize. These activities allow children to process their grief in a way that feels natural to them.

It's important to monitor for signs of complicated grief, which may indicate that a child needs professional help. Prolonged depression or anxiety, persistent nightmares, and significant changes in behavior or academic performance are red flags. If a child is consistently withdrawn, exhibiting aggressive behavior, or struggling with schoolwork, it may be time to seek the assistance of a counselor or therapist. These professionals are trained to help children navigate their grief and can provide strategies and support tailored to their developmental stage and individual needs.

Encouraging healthy coping mechanisms can help children deal with their grief in constructive ways. Drawing or painting their feelings can be particularly therapeutic. These activities allow children to express emotions that they might not yet have the words for. Participating in physical activities like sports can also provide an outlet for pent-up energy and stress. The physical exertion of play can help release endorphins, which improve mood and reduce anxiety. Writing letters or stories about their loved one is another powerful coping strategy. These letters can be a way for children to maintain a connection with the person they've lost, helping them to process their feelings and memories in a tangible form.

Consider the story of a young girl named Lily, who lost her father unexpectedly. Her mother noticed that Lily became increasingly quiet and withdrawn, avoiding activities she once loved. To help her cope, they established a routine that included a daily drawing session where Lily could express her feelings through art. They also continued with her ballet classes, which provided a sense of normalcy and an outlet for her emotions. Over time, Lily began to open up more verbally and through her drawings, gradually improving her emotional state.

Another example is of a boy named Max, who lost his older brother in a car accident. Max's parents encouraged him to join a local soccer team, knowing how much he loved the sport. They also set aside time each week for the family to write letters to his brother, which they placed in a special memory box. These activities gave Max a way to channel his grief and maintain a connection with his brother while also providing the physical and emotional support he needed.

By maintaining consistent routines, offering emotional support, monitoring for signs of complicated grief, and encouraging healthy coping mechanisms, you can provide a supportive environment for a grieving child. These strategies help create a sense of stability and security, allowing children to navigate their grief healthily and constructively.

AGE-APPROPRIATE ACTIVITIES FOR GRIEVING CHILDREN

When it comes to helping younger children, ages 3 to 7, process their grief, tangible activities can be incredibly beneficial. Creating a memory box with mementos of the loved one can be a comforting and interactive way for them to remember. Collect items like photos, favorite toys, or small keepsakes that remind them of the person who has passed. These physical objects can provide a sense of connection and continuity. Drawing pictures of their favorite memories is another excellent activity. Give them crayons and paper, and encourage them to draw scenes or moments they shared with their loved one. This allows them to express their feelings visually, which can sometimes be easier than using words. Reading storybooks about loss together can also be soothing. Books like "The Invisible String" by Patrice Karst or "The Goodbye Book" by Todd Parr can help them understand their emotions and feel less alone in their grief.

For school-aged children, ages 8 to 12, writing a letter to the loved one can be a powerful way to process their feelings. Encourage them to write about what they miss, what they loved about the person, or even things they wish they could have said. This exercise provides a safe space for emotional expression. Making a scrapbook of photos and memories can also be a cathartic activity. Provide materials like photos, stickers, and colorful paper, and help them create a scrapbook that celebrates the life of their loved one. This can be a project you work on together, fostering a sense of connection and shared memories. Engaging in role-play to express emotions is another helpful activity. Provide costumes or props and let them act out different scenarios. This can be a fun and creative way for them to explore complex emotions and gain a sense of control over their feelings.

Teenagers, ages 13 to 18, often benefit from activities that allow for more introspection and personal expression. Keeping a grief journal is a valuable tool for older children. Encourage them to write regularly about their thoughts and feelings and any memories they wish to preserve. This practice can help them process their grief over time and track their emotional journey. Creating a digital memorial or tribute video is another activity that resonates well with teens. They can compile photos, videos, and music to create a tribute to their loved one. This project not only honors the deceased but also allows them to use technology, which is often more engaging for this age group. Participating in group discussions or support groups can provide a sense of community. Encourage them to join groups where they can share their experiences and hear from others who are going through similar situations. This can help them feel understood and less isolated.

Incorporating family activities can create a sense of unity and support. Planting a tree or garden in memory of the loved one is a meaningful and lasting tribute. Choose a spot in your yard or a community garden, and involve everyone in the planting process. Watching the tree grow can symbolize the enduring presence of the loved one in your lives. Organizing a family remembrance ceremony can also be a powerful way to honor the deceased. This could be a simple gathering where each family member shares a memory or reads a poem. Lighting candles, playing their favorite songs, or displaying photos can make the ceremony even more special. Lastly, sharing stories and memories during family gatherings can keep the memory of the loved one alive. Set aside time during meals or special occasions to talk about them, laugh at the funny moments, and cherish the love you all shared.

INTEGRATING GRIEF SUPPORT IN DAILY ROUTINES

Incorporating grief support into a child's daily routines can provide a sense of stability and continuity. One practical way to do this is by having morning check-ins to discuss feelings. These can be as simple as asking, "How are you feeling today?" over breakfast. This small act can set the tone for the day and let your child know that it's okay to talk about their emotions. Regular bedtime routines that include talking about the day can also be incredibly soothing. Before turning out the lights, spend a few minutes discussing what happened during the day, how they felt, and any thoughts they want to share. This ritual provides emotional support and helps them process their feelings before sleep, making it easier to rest.

Setting aside time for creative expression is another valuable way to integrate grief support. Encourage activities like drawing, painting, or writing. These creative outlets allow children to express emotions that might be too difficult to articulate. Create a dedicated space in your home for these activities, stocked with supplies like paper, crayons, and paints. This space can become a safe haven where your child can retreat whenever they need to express themselves. In our home, we set up a small art corner in the living room. It became a go-to spot for our niece to draw pictures of her Grandpa, helping her keep his memory alive while processing her grief.

Rituals and traditions play a crucial role in helping children cope with loss. Simple acts like lighting a candle at dinner in memory of the loved one can provide a sense of connection and continuity. This small, daily ritual can be a comforting reminder that the person they miss is still a part of their lives. Celebrating the loved one's birthday with a special activity can also be meaningful. Whether it's baking their favorite cake, visiting a place they loved, or engaging in an activity they enjoyed, these rituals honor the loved one's memory and provide a structured way to acknowledge their absence. For instance, every year on my father's birthday, we gather to cook his favorite meal and share stories about him. This tradition has become a cherished way to keep his spirit alive in our family.

Open communication within the family is vital for navigating grief. Regular family meetings can be an excellent way to discuss emotions and support each other. These meetings don't have to be formal; they can be casual gatherings where everyone has a chance to speak and share their feelings. Encourage siblings to talk about their experiences and emotions. This openness fosters a supportive environment where everyone feels heard and understood. In our family, we started having weekly "family check-ins" where we would sit together and talk about how we were feeling. These sessions allowed everyone to express their grief and support each other, strengthening our family bonds.

Consistent emotional support is crucial for helping a child navigate their grief. Being available to listen whenever the child needs to talk is one of the most important things you can do. Make it clear that they can come to you at any time with their feelings, questions, or concerns. Offering reassurance and comfort is equally important. Simple affirmations like "It's okay to feel sad" or "I'm here for you" can provide immense comfort. Physical gestures, such as hugging or holding hands, can also convey a sense of security and love. Consistency in your emotional support helps build a foundation of trust, making it easier for the child to open up and share their feelings.

In our home, we made a point to be emotionally available at all times. Whether it was a late-night conversation or a quiet moment during a car ride, we ensured that our niece knew she could talk to us whenever she needed. This openness helped her feel supported and understood, allowing her to navigate her grief in a healthy way. Integrating these practices into daily routines, creating new rituals, maintaining open communication, and providing consistent emotional support are all ways to help a child cope with the loss of a loved one.

RESOURCES FOR PARENTS AND CAREGIVERS

When it comes to supporting grieving children, having the right resources can make a significant difference. Books and literature can provide valuable guidance and comfort. One highly recommended book is "The Invisible String" by Patrice Karst. This touching story explains how an invisible string connects us to our loved ones, no matter the distance or separation. It's a beautiful way to help children understand that the bond with their loved one remains even after death. Another excellent resource is "When Dinosaurs Die: A Guide to Understanding Death" by Laurie Krasny Brown and Marc Brown. This book offers straightforward explanations about death and grief, making it easier for children to grasp these complex topics. It's filled with engaging illustrations and covers various aspects of death, from the emotions involved to what happens at funerals.

Support groups and counseling services are invaluable for grieving children and their families. Local support groups for children and teens provide a safe space where they can share their feelings and connect with others who understand their experience. These groups often use age-appropriate activities and discussions to help children process their grief. Grief counseling services for children can offer personalized support. Counselors specializing in child grief can provide strategies tailored to a child's developmental stage and individual needs. They create a safe environment where children can express their emotions and work through their grief with professional guidance.

Online resources and forums also offer valuable support. Websites like the Dougy Center and GriefShare provide a wealth of information and resources for grieving families. The Dougy Center offers articles, activities, and support group listings specifically for children and teens. GriefShare provides online support groups and resources for families navigating grief. These platforms offer flexibility, allowing families to access support from the comfort of their own homes. Online forums for parents of grieving children can also be a lifeline. These forums allow parents to share their experiences, seek advice, and find comfort in knowing they are not alone. Engaging with a community of parents who are facing similar challenges can provide emotional support and practical tips for helping their children cope.

Community resources can provide additional layers of support. Community centers often offer grief workshops and support groups. These workshops can provide practical tools and strategies for coping with grief, as well as opportunities to connect with others in the community. School counselors and support programs are also valuable resources. Many schools have counselors trained in grief support who can provide individual or group counseling for students. These programs can help ensure that children receive the support they need during school hours, making it easier for them to stay engaged in their education while coping with their loss.

To illustrate the impact of these resources, let's consider the story of a family who lost their father. The mother, seeking ways to support her two young children, turned to various resources. She started by reading "The Invisible String" to her kids, which helped them understand that their connection to their dad remained even though he wasn't physically present. She also enrolled them in a local support group for children, where they participated in activities designed to help them express their grief. Additionally, she found comfort and advice through an online forum for parents of grieving children. The combination of these resources provided a comprehensive support system, helping the family navigate their grief together.

Having access to a variety of resources can make a significant difference in helping children cope with the loss of a loved one. Books, support groups, counseling services, online resources, and community programs all offer unique forms of support that can address different aspects of grief. By utilizing these resources, parents and caregivers can provide the comprehensive support their children need to navigate this challenging time.

CHAPTER 7
CULTURAL AND SPIRITUAL PERSPECTIVES ON GRIEF

GRIEF PRACTICES IN DIFFERENT CULTURES

I remember attending a Day of the Dead celebration in Mexico. The air was filled with the scent of marigolds and vibrant altars adorned with photographs, candles, and the deceased's favorite foods lined the streets. Families gathered to honor and remember their departed loved ones, transforming grief into a colorful and communal celebration. The experience was both moving and enlightening, revealing how different cultures navigate the complexities of loss.

The Mexican Día de los Muertos, or Day of the Dead, is a poignant example of how traditional mourning practices can help individuals cope with loss. Celebrated on November 1st and 2nd, this holiday combines Indigenous Mexican traditions with elements of Christianity, creating a unique blend that honors the dead while celebrating life. Families build ofrendas, or altars, in their homes, decorated with marigolds, sugar skulls, and the favorite foods and beverages of the deceased. These altars serve as a way to welcome the spirits back to the world of the living, creating a sense of connection and continuity. The community aspect of this celebration is profound, as families come together to share stories, memories, and rituals, transforming grief into a communal act of remembrance.

In Ireland, wakes are a traditional mourning practice that brings the community together to support the bereaved family. An Irish wake typically occurs in the deceased's home, where friends and family gather to pay their respects, share stories, and offer comfort. The atmosphere is often a mix of somber reflection and lively celebration, reflecting the dual nature of grief and joy. Songs are sung, toasts are made, and memories are shared, creating a space where grief is acknowledged and shared. This communal support is integral to the grieving process, providing a network of care and connection. The wake serves as a bridge between the living and the dead, honoring the life of the deceased while offering solace to those left behind.

New Orleans jazz funerals are another unique cultural expression of grief. Rooted in African and French traditions, these funerals blend music, celebration, and mourning in a powerful display of community support. The funeral procession typically begins with a somber dirge played by a brass band, reflecting the sorrow of loss. As the procession moves away from the burial site, the music shifts to lively jazz tunes, celebrating the life of the deceased and the belief in an afterlife. This transformation from sorrow to joy encapsulates the resilience of the human spirit and the healing power of community. The jazz funeral is a testament to the belief that life should be celebrated, even in the face of death, and that music can provide a path to healing.

The role of community in mourning is evident in many cultures, where collective support is integral to the grieving process. In many African cultures, mourning is a communal activity, with extended family and community members coming together to support the bereaved. Rituals such as communal meals, storytelling, and collective prayers help create a sense of solidarity and shared mourning. These practices reinforce the idea that grief is not a solitary journey but a shared experience that binds the community together. Similarly, Indigenous communities often have community-based rituals that honor the deceased and support the grieving family. These rituals may include feasts, dances, and ceremonies that connect the living with their ancestors, creating a sense of continuity and belonging.

Cultural expressions of grief are diverse and deeply rooted in tradition. The Japanese Obon Festival, for example, is a Buddhist event that honors the spirits of ancestors. This multi-day festival involves cleaning ancestors' graves, offering food and flowers, and performing traditional dances called Bon Odori. Lanterns are lit to guide the spirits back to the physical world, creating a beautiful and serene atmosphere. The festival concludes with the lighting of floating lanterns or bonfires to send the spirits back to the afterlife. The Obon Festival is a time for families to come together, honor their heritage, and find comfort in communal rituals.

Jewish Shiva practices are another example of how cultural rituals can provide structure and support during grief. Shiva, which means "seven" in Hebrew, refers to the seven-day mourning period observed by the deceased's immediate family. During Shiva, mourners stay at home and receive visitors who come to offer condolences, share memories, and provide support. The community plays a vital role in this practice, bringing food, helping with daily tasks, and creating a space where grief is openly expressed and shared. The rituals of Shiva, such as covering mirrors, sitting on low stools, and reciting prayers, provide a framework for mourning that honors the deceased and supports the mourners.

Cultural symbols and artifacts also play a significant role in expressing grief and remembrance. In Chinese funerals, mourners traditionally wear white clothing, symbolizing purity and respect for the deceased. This practice contrasts with Western cultures, where black armbands or clothing are commonly worn to signify mourning. These symbols serve as visual representations of grief, creating a shared language of loss and remembrance. They also provide a sense of order and ritual, helping individuals navigate the emotional landscape of grief.

Reflection Section: Exploring Cultural Practices

Take a moment to reflect on your own cultural background and any mourning practices you have experienced or observed. How have these practices helped you or others cope with loss? Consider writing down your thoughts and memories and exploring how cultural traditions have shaped your understanding of grief and healing. If you are open to it, you might also research and incorporate new practices from different cultures that resonate with you, creating a personalized approach to mourning that honors both your heritage and your unique journey.

RELIGIOUS PERSPECTIVES ON MOURNING

Christian mourning traditions often center around the belief in eternal life, providing solace to those grieving a loss. Funeral services are a cornerstone of these rituals, offering a structured way to say goodbye. A service typically includes prayers, hymns, and scripture readings that emphasize hope and resurrection. The eulogy is a heartfelt tribute to the deceased, often filled with personal anecdotes and reflections on their life. This moment allows family and friends to share their memories, creating a space for collective mourning. The concept of eternal life is deeply comforting to many Christians. It reassures them that death is not the end but a transition to a new, eternal existence. This belief helps to alleviate the fear of death and provides a sense of peace, knowing that their loved ones are in a better place. The graveside service often reinforces this message, focusing on the defeat of the grave and the promise of eternal life.

In Islam, mourning practices are deeply rooted in religious teachings and traditions. The Janazah, or funeral prayer, is critical to Islamic mourning. It is performed in a congregation, often at a mosque, and emphasizes the community's role in supporting the bereaved. The prayer is a plea for mercy and forgiveness for the deceased, reflecting the importance of compassion and solidarity. Following the Janazah, the body is buried in a simple grave, facing Mecca. The 40-day mourning period, known as the "Iddah," allows the family to grieve while receiving support from their community. During this time, it is customary for loved ones to visit the family, offering prayers and words of comfort. Charity, or Sadaqah, is also a significant aspect of mourning in Islam. Giving to those in need in memory of the deceased is considered a virtuous act, believed to benefit both the giver and the departed soul. This practice reinforces the idea of community support and compassion, channeling grief into positive action.

Jewish mourning practices are rich with rituals that offer structure and support during a time of loss. Sitting Shiva is perhaps the most well-known of these practices. Shiva, which means "seven" in Hebrew, refers to the seven-day mourning period observed by the immediate family of the deceased. During this time, mourners stay at home and receive visitors who come to offer condolences, share memories, and provide support. The community plays a vital role in this practice, bringing food, helping with daily tasks, and creating a space where grief is openly expressed and shared. The Mourner's Kaddish, a prayer recited daily during Shiva, is a powerful expression of faith and continuity, emphasizing the sanctity of life. Yahrzeit, the anniversary of the death, is another significant observance. Each year on the anniversary, a candle is lit, and the Kaddish is recited in memory of the loved one. These rituals provide a framework for mourning that honors the deceased and supports the mourners.

Hindu perspectives on mourning are deeply intertwined with beliefs about the soul and reincarnation. Cremation is the preferred method of handling the body, as it is believed to free the soul from its earthly ties. The cremation ceremony is a solemn event, often performed by the eldest son or a close male relative. The ashes are typically scattered in a sacred river, symbolizing the soul's return to the elements and its journey towards rebirth. Following the cremation, a 13-day mourning period, known as "Shraddha," is observed. During this time, the family performs daily rituals to honor the deceased and support the soul's journey to the afterlife. These rituals include offering food and water to the ancestors, reciting prayers, and lighting lamps. Ancestor worship during Pitru Paksha, a specific fortnight in the Hindu lunar calendar, is another key practice. During this time, offerings are made to deceased ancestors, seeking their blessings and ensuring their peace in the afterlife. These practices reflect the Hindu belief in the cyclical nature of life and death, providing a sense of continuity and connection to the past.

SPIRITUAL RITUALS FOR HEALING

Spiritual rituals can offer profound comfort and healing during the grieving process. These rituals are practices that connect you to something greater than yourself, providing a sense of peace and stability. They can be as simple as lighting a candle or as elaborate as a full ceremony. The importance of spiritual rituals lies in their ability to create a sacred space where you can honor your emotions, reflect on your loss, and find moments of solace. These rituals provide a structured way to process grief, allowing you to navigate the complexities of loss with a sense of purpose and connection.

Nature-based rituals have long been used to find solace and healing. Forest bathing, or Shinrin-yoku, is a Japanese practice that involves immersing yourself in the forest, allowing the sights, sounds, and smells of nature to envelop you. This practice is believed to reduce stress, improve mood, and enhance overall well-being. Walking slowly through the forest, focusing on the rustling leaves, the chirping birds, and the gentle breeze can create a calming and meditative experience. Water rituals, such as cleansing ceremonies in rivers or lakes, are another way to connect with nature. These rituals often involve symbolic acts of washing away grief and renewing one's spirit. The act of immersing yourself in water, feeling its cool embrace, can be a powerful metaphor for cleansing and rebirth.

Meditation and mindfulness practices also serve as spiritual rituals that can help you cope with grief. Guided meditation sessions provide a structured way to focus your mind, often leading you through visualizations that promote relaxation and emotional healing. These sessions can be done in person, through apps, or online videos, offering flexibility to fit into your routine. Mindful breathing exercises are another simple yet effective practice. By focusing on your breath, you can anchor yourself in the present moment, reducing anxiety and creating a sense of calm. Visualization techniques, such as imagining a peaceful place or envisioning yourself surrounded by light, can also provide comfort and help you process your emotions. These practices encourage you to be present, to acknowledge your feelings without judgment, and to find moments of peace amid the turmoil of grief.

Personal spiritual rituals can be deeply meaningful and unique to each individual. Lighting candles in memory of the deceased is a common practice that creates a sacred space for reflection and connection. The soft glow of the candlelight can symbolize the enduring presence of your loved one, offering comfort and a sense of continuity. Creating an altar or sacred space at home can also provide a focal point for your grief. This space can be adorned with photographs, meaningful objects, and items that remind you of your loved one. Spending time at the altar, saying prayers, or simply sitting in silence can create a sense of peace and connection. Daily affirmations and prayers can also be powerful spiritual practices. By repeating positive affirmations or reciting prayers that resonate with you, you can create a routine that supports your emotional and spiritual well-being.

I remember a woman who found solace in lighting a candle every evening in memory of her late husband. She would sit by the candle, say a quiet prayer, and reflect on their time together. This simple act became a nightly ritual that brought her comfort and a sense of connection. Another person I spoke with created a small altar in their home, filled with photographs and mementos of their loved one. They would spend a few moments each day at the altar, expressing their thoughts and feelings. This practice provided a dedicated space for their grief, helping them process their emotions. Daily affirmations also played a significant role in their healing. By starting each day with positive affirmations, they were able to cultivate a sense of hope and resilience.

These personal stories highlight the power of spiritual rituals in providing comfort and healing. Whether through nature-based practices, meditation and mindfulness, or personal rituals, these practices offer a way to honor your grief, connect with your loved one, and find moments of peace. They provide a structured and meaningful way to navigate the complexities of loss, creating a sense of purpose and connection.

INCORPORATING CULTURAL TRADITIONS IN GRIEF RECOVERY

Embracing your cultural heritage during the grieving process can offer profound comfort and support. The rituals and traditions passed down through generations serve as a bridge between the past and the present, creating a sense of continuity and connection. When you incorporate these traditions into your grief recovery, you strengthen family bonds and find solace in familiar practices. These rituals are more than mere customs; they are touchstones that ground you in your identity and provide a framework for expressing your grief. By engaging in these practices, you honor your loved one while also reaffirming your place within your cultural lineage.

There are many practical ways to integrate cultural traditions into your daily life as you navigate grief. Preparing traditional meals in honor of your loved one is a simple yet meaningful act. Cooking their favorite dishes brings back cherished memories and allows you to share those memories with family and friends. Food has a unique way of connecting people, and sharing a meal can become a ritual of remembrance. Participating in cultural festivals and ceremonies is another way to keep your heritage alive. These events often include communal activities that foster a sense of belonging and support. Engaging in these traditions helps you feel connected to your roots and provides a sense of normalcy amid the upheaval of loss.

Storytelling is a powerful tool in preserving cultural heritage and coping with grief. Sharing family stories and legends can provide comfort and a sense of continuity. These narratives are a way to keep the memory of your loved one alive, passing down their legacy to future generations. Recording oral histories can be an enriching project, capturing the voices and stories of family members. This practice not only preserves valuable cultural knowledge but also creates a lasting tribute to those who have passed. By engaging in storytelling, you create a shared space for grief and healing, allowing everyone to contribute their memories and experiences.

I recall a friend who lost her mother and found solace in preparing traditional meals that her mother used to cook. Each dish was a labor of love, filling her home with familiar scents and tastes that brought back fond memories. She invited family and friends to join her, turning these meals into gatherings of remembrance and connection. Another person I spoke with found comfort in participating in cultural festivals that celebrated their heritage. These events provided a sense of community and belonging, reminding them that they were not alone in their grief.

One man shared how storytelling became a vital part of his grief recovery. After losing his father, he started recording conversations with his relatives, capturing their memories and stories. This project became a cherished family archive, preserving the legacy of his father and other ancestors. He found that listening to these recordings offered a sense of closeness and continuity, easing the pain of loss. The lessons he learned from these stories also provided valuable insights and guidance, helping him navigate his own life challenges.

Incorporating cultural traditions into your grief recovery is not just about following rituals; it's about creating a space where you can honor your loved one and find comfort in your heritage. These practices allow you to connect with your roots, strengthen family bonds, and find solace in familiar customs. Whether through preparing traditional meals, participating in cultural events, or engaging in storytelling, these traditions offer a meaningful way to navigate the complexities of grief. They provide a framework for expressing your emotions, honoring your loved one, and finding a sense of peace and continuity in the midst of loss.

FINDING MEANING AND PURPOSE IN SPIRITUALITY

The search for meaning in the wake of loss is often a deeply personal and profound journey. Spirituality can play a significant role in helping individuals find purpose and understanding after a loved one has passed. When you're grappling with overwhelming grief, spirituality offers a framework for making sense of your emotions and experiences. It provides a lens through which you can view your loss, helping you to find acceptance and peace. This search for understanding isn't about finding definitive answers but rather about discovering a sense of purpose and connection that helps you navigate your grief.

Spiritual growth can emerge from the depths of grief. The process of mourning can lead to a deeper understanding of oneself and one's beliefs. As you confront your loss, you may find that your spiritual beliefs evolve, offering new insights and perspectives. This growth isn't always linear or easy, but it can be a source of strength and resilience. Many people find that their spiritual practices become more meaningful during times of grief, offering solace and a sense of continuity. Engaging in rituals, prayers, or meditative practices can provide a sense of structure and purpose, helping you to process your emotions and find moments of peace.

Various spiritual philosophies offer guidance on finding meaning in grief. Existential perspectives on loss emphasize the importance of creating meaning in the face of suffering. Existentialism teaches that life is inherently without meaning, but it is up to each individual to create their own purpose. This philosophy can be empowering, encouraging you to find your own path through grief and to create meaning from your experiences. Buddhist teachings on impermanence also offer valuable insights. Buddhism teaches that everything is constantly changing and that attachment to the way things were is the root of suffering. By accepting the impermanent nature of life, you can find comfort in the understanding that your grief, like all things, will change and evolve over time. These teachings encourage mindfulness and presence, helping you to focus on the here and now rather than being consumed by the past or the future.

Faith communities can provide a robust support system and a sense of purpose during times of grief. Involvement in church or temple activities can offer a sense of belonging and connection. These communities often provide structured support, such as grief counseling, support groups, and communal prayers. Being part of a faith community means having a network of people who share your beliefs and who can provide comfort and understanding. Volunteering and community service within these communities can also be a powerful way to channel your grief into positive action. Helping others can provide a sense of purpose and fulfillment, reminding you that even in the midst of your pain, you can make a difference in the lives of others.

Personal stories of spiritual growth can be incredibly inspiring. I recall speaking with a woman named Maria, who found deep solace in her faith after losing her husband. She joined her church's grief support group, where she met others who had experienced similar losses. Through these connections, she found comfort and understanding. Maria also began volunteering at her church, helping to organize community events and support services. This involvement gave her a sense of purpose and helped her to feel connected to her husband's memory in a meaningful way. "Volunteering gave me a reason to get up in the morning," she said. "It made me feel like I was honoring his memory by helping others."

Another individual, James, turned to Buddhist teachings after the sudden death of his sister. He found the concept of impermanence to be particularly comforting. "Understanding that everything changes, including my grief, helped me to find peace," he shared. James began practicing mindfulness and meditation, which provided a sense of calm and presence. He also joined a local meditation group, where he found a supportive community of like-minded individuals. This practice became a cornerstone of his healing journey, helping him to navigate his grief with greater resilience and understanding.

LEARNING FROM GLOBAL GRIEF PRACTICES

Exploring global grief practices can offer new insights and approaches to your own grieving process. Understanding how different cultures navigate loss can enrich your perspective and provide you with unique tools for coping. By learning about these practices, you might find commonalities that resonate with your own experiences, as well as differences that offer new ways to understand and express your grief. This knowledge can help you feel less isolated, knowing that grief is a universal experience that transcends cultural boundaries. It can also provide innovative methods for honoring your loved one and finding comfort in your grief.

One unique practice is the Tibetan Sky Burial, a traditional funeral method in which the body is placed on a mountaintop to decompose naturally or be eaten by scavenging birds. This practice is rooted in the Buddhist belief in the impermanence of life and the importance of returning the body to nature. The Sky Burial symbolizes the release of the soul from the physical body, allowing it to continue its journey in the cycle of life and death. While this practice is specific to Tibetan culture, its underlying principles of impermanence and natural return can offer valuable insights into accepting the transience of life and finding peace in the natural order.

In South Korea, Jesa ceremonies are held to honor ancestors. These rituals typically involve preparing a table with food offerings, burning incense, and performing bowing rites. The ceremonies are conducted on the anniversary of the ancestor's death and during major holidays. Jesa serves as a way to maintain a connection with deceased family members, honoring their memory and seeking their blessings. This practice highlights the importance of family bonds and continuity, providing a structured way to remember and celebrate loved ones. By incorporating elements of Jesa, such as preparing special meals or setting aside time to honor your loved one, you can create a sense of tradition and connection that supports your grieving process.

Ghanaian Fantasy Coffins are another fascinating example of unique grief practices. In Ghana, coffins are often elaborately designed to represent the deceased's profession, interests, or status. These coffins can take the shape of anything from a fish to symbolize a fisherman to an airplane for a pilot. The practice reflects the belief that the afterlife is a continuation of this life, and the coffin serves as a tribute to the deceased's identity and achievements. While you may not adopt the exact practice of Fantasy Coffins, the idea of personalizing memorials to reflect your loved one's life can be deeply meaningful. Creating a tribute that honors their passions and accomplishments can provide comfort and a sense of celebration.

Adopting elements from global grief practices can provide comfort and healing by allowing you to create new rituals that resonate with your personal needs. These practices can be adapted to fit your cultural context and personal preferences, offering a sense of continuity and connection. For instance, you might incorporate the idea of offerings from Jesa by preparing your loved one's favorite foods on special occasions. Or, you might find solace in the concept of impermanence from Tibetan Sky Burials, using it as a reminder to accept the natural cycle of life and death.

I once spoke with a woman who integrated elements of various cultural practices into her grieving process. After losing her father, she found comfort in the Tibetan concept of impermanence, which helped her accept the changes in her life. She also adopted the practice of setting up a small altar at home, inspired by Jesa ceremonies, where she placed her father's photograph and favorite items. This altar became a space for her to reflect and connect with his memory. "It made me feel like he was still part of my daily life," she said. Another person I met personalized a memorial for her late husband by creating a garden that reflected his love for nature, inspired by the idea of Fantasy Coffins. She planted his favorite flowers and included a small plaque with a tribute to his life. "Tending to the garden helped me feel close to him," she shared.

These stories illustrate how integrating elements from global grief practices can provide new ways to honor your loved one and find comfort in your grief. By exploring and adapting these practices, you can create personalized rituals that resonate with your unique needs and cultural background. This approach not only enriches your grieving process but also offers a sense of connection and continuity with the broader human experience of loss and remembrance.

CHAPTER 8
MOVING FORWARD AND FINDING HOPE

I remember a crisp, clear morning when I decided to take a walk in the park. It had been months since Brittney's sudden passing, and the world still felt heavy. As I wandered along the path, I noticed a small tree, newly planted, with a plaque beneath it. It read, "In memory of Sarah, who brought light to all who knew her." I stood there, absorbed in the moment, feeling a strange mix of sorrow and solace. Then, I realized the power of resilience—the ability to find strength and hope, even when the world seems bleak. This motivated me to name a star for Brittney.

BUILDING RESILIENCE THROUGH GRIEF

Resilience is the capacity to adapt and grow in response to loss and traumatic events. It's not about avoiding pain or pretending everything is fine. Instead, resilience allows you to confront your grief, process it, and emerge stronger. Dr. Arielle Schwartz, a psychologist specializing in trauma recovery, describes resilience as finding strength and courage amidst adversity. Resilience is crucial during the grieving process because it helps you navigate the intense emotions and challenges that come with loss. It provides a framework for healing, allowing you to move forward while honoring your loved one's memory.

Building resilience involves changing negative thought patterns, a process known as cognitive restructuring. This means identifying and challenging unhelpful thoughts, replacing them with more balanced and constructive ones. For instance, instead of thinking, "I'll never get through this," you might remind yourself, "This is incredibly hard, but I have the strength to cope." Developing a growth mindset can also foster resilience. This involves viewing challenges as opportunities for growth rather than insurmountable obstacles. Embrace the idea that while grief is painful, it can also lead to personal growth and a deeper understanding of life's fragility and beauty.

Practicing self-compassion is another key strategy for building resilience. Be kind and gentle with yourself during this difficult time. Acknowledge your pain and allow yourself to grieve without judgment. This might involve speaking to yourself as you would to a dear friend, offering words of comfort and understanding. Remember, it's okay to feel a range of emotions, and it's important to give yourself permission to grieve in your own way and at your own pace.

Social support networks play a vital role in building resilience. Strengthening relationships with family and friends can provide a sense of connection and belonging. Share your feelings and experiences with those you trust and allow them to support you. Community groups can also offer valuable support. Joining a grief support group or participating in community activities can connect you with others who understand your pain and can provide empathy and encouragement. These connections help to normalize your experiences and offer a sense of solidarity.

Consider the story of Lisa, who lost her husband unexpectedly. She found solace in a local support group for widows. "Sharing my story with others who had experienced similar losses made me feel less alone," she said. "We supported each other through the darkest times." Lisa also began practicing self-compassion by journaling her thoughts and feelings. "Writing became a way to process my emotions and offer myself kindness," she explained. Over time, she noticed a shift in her mindset, from feeling overwhelmed by her grief to finding small moments of hope and strength.

Another example is John, who lost his brother in a tragic accident. Initially, John felt consumed by anger and guilt. Through cognitive restructuring, he began to challenge these negative thoughts, reminding himself that the accident was not his fault. He also reached out to friends and family, strengthening his support network. "Talking to my friends and family helped me process my grief," John shared. "Their support made a huge difference." John also joined a community group focused on outdoor activities, finding comfort in nature and physical activity. "Hiking with the group gave me a sense of peace and connection," he said. "It was a way to honor my brother's memory while taking care of myself."

Building resilience through grief involves a combination of cognitive restructuring, developing a growth mindset, practicing self-compassion, and seeking social support. These strategies can help you navigate the complexities of grief and find strength and hope in the midst of loss. Remember, resilience is not about avoiding pain but about finding ways to adapt, grow, and move forward while keeping your loved one's memory alive.

FINDING NEW PURPOSE AND MEANING

Finding a new purpose after the loss of a loved one can be a lifeline. It's a way to anchor yourself amid the storm of grief. Purpose plays a crucial role in emotional well-being by providing a sense of direction and motivation. When you have something meaningful to focus on, it can help alleviate some of the emptiness and despair that often accompanies loss. It gives you a reason to get out of bed in the morning, to take small steps forward each day. Purpose doesn't erase the pain, but it offers a way to navigate through it, to find moments of light in the darkness.

Discovering a new purpose can begin with reflecting on your passions and interests. Think about the activities that once brought you joy or the causes that have always mattered to you. These can serve as clues to finding a new direction. Setting new personal and professional goals is another way to create a sense of purpose. These goals don't have to be monumental; they can be as simple as learning a new skill, starting a hobby, or pursuing a new career path. Volunteering and community involvement can also provide a profound sense of purpose. Helping others can be incredibly healing, offering a way to give back and make a positive impact in the world.

Engaging in exercises for self-discovery can help you identify new purposes. Journaling prompts focused on self-reflection can be a powerful tool. Ask yourself questions like, "What activities make me feel alive?" or "What causes am I passionate about?" Writing down your thoughts can bring clarity and insight. Vision board creation is another exercise that can help you visualize your new purpose. Gather images, quotes, and symbols that resonate with you and arrange them on a board. This visual representation can serve as a daily reminder of your goals and aspirations. Meditation and mindfulness practices can also aid in self-discovery. Taking time to sit quietly and focus on your breath can help you connect with your inner self and uncover what truly matters to you.

Consider the story of Maria, who lost her husband, Tom, to a sudden heart attack. Initially, Maria felt lost and aimless. She began journaling her thoughts and feelings, which led her to rediscover her love for gardening. Maria decided to create a community garden in Tom's memory, providing fresh produce for her neighborhood. "Gardening became my therapy," she explained. "It gave me a sense of purpose and a way to honor Tom's memory." Through her work in the garden, Maria found a new direction and a way to channel her grief into something positive.

Another example is David, who lost his daughter, Emily, in a car accident. David struggled to find meaning in his life after her death. He started volunteering at a local youth center, where he mentored teenagers. "Helping these kids gave me a reason to keep going," David shared. "It felt like I was making a difference, and in a way, it honored Emily's spirit." Volunteering provided David with a new sense of purpose and helped him find a way to move forward while keeping his daughter's memory alive.

These stories illustrate how finding a new purpose can help you navigate through grief. By reflecting on your passions, setting new goals, and engaging in community involvement, you can create a sense of direction and motivation. Exercises like journaling, vision board creation, and mindfulness practices can aid in this process. Remember, discovering a new purpose is a personal journey, and it's important to be patient and compassionate with yourself as you explore new paths.

CREATING LASTING MEMORIALS FOR LOVED ONES

Creating lasting memorials for loved ones who have passed away is a meaningful way to honor their memory and provide a sense of connection. These memorials serve as tangible reminders of the love and life shared, offering comfort and a place to focus your grief. They allow you to keep the memory alive, preserving your loved one's legacy in a way that can be revisited and cherished over time. Memorials also provide an opportunity to celebrate the life and impact of the deceased, turning mourning into a tribute that honors their uniqueness.

One beautiful way to create a lasting memorial is by planting a tree or garden in your loved one's memory. This living tribute can be a place of solace and reflection, where you can feel connected to your loved one as you watch the plants grow and change with the seasons. Choose plants that held special meaning for them or that symbolize qualities you admired in them. To get started, select a location that will be accessible and meaningful to you. Prepare the soil and choose plants that are well-suited to the climate and conditions of the area. Plant the tree or garden with care and consider adding a small plaque or marker to signify the dedication.

Another meaningful option is creating a scholarship fund in your loved one's name. This can turn your grief into an opportunity to help others, ensuring that their legacy lives on through the education and growth of future generations. To establish a scholarship, first decide on the criteria for the award, such as academic achievement or financial need. Contact local schools, universities, or community organizations to partner with them in setting up the fund. You may need to create a formal application process and establish a selection committee. Fundraising can be done through community events, online campaigns, or personal contributions. Once the scholarship is established, you can take pride in knowing that your loved one's memory is helping others achieve their dreams.

Designing a memorial plaque or bench is another way to honor your loved one. This can be placed in a location that was significant to them, such as a favorite park or garden. Contact local authorities or organizations to obtain permission and discuss the necessary steps. Work with a designer to create a plaque or bench that includes a meaningful inscription or quote. Once installed, this memorial can serve as a place for you and others to sit, reflect, and remember the person you lost.

Organizing an annual remembrance event is a powerful way to gather friends and family to celebrate your loved one's life. This could be a memorial walk, a charity event, or a simple gathering at a meaningful location. Start by choosing a date that holds significance, such as their birthday or the anniversary of their passing. Plan activities that honor their memory, such as sharing stories, playing their favorite music, or participating in a hobby they loved. Invite those who were close to your loved one and encourage them to contribute to the event. This annual tradition can become a cherished time for collective remembrance and healing.

Consider the story of Emily, who lost her father suddenly. She established a scholarship fund in his name at the local high school to honor his love for education. Each year, the scholarship is awarded to a student who shares her father's passion for learning and community service. "Knowing that my dad's legacy is helping students achieve their dreams brings me comfort," Emily shared. The scholarship fund has become a source of pride and a way for Emily to stay connected to her father's values.

John, who lost his wife, created a beautiful garden in her memory. He planted her favorite flowers and added a bench with a plaque that reads, "In loving memory of Sarah, whose beauty and kindness bloomed in every season." The garden has become a sanctuary for John, a place where he feels close to his wife and finds solace in nature. "Tending to the garden is my way of honoring Sarah's love for life," he explained.

These examples illustrate how creating lasting memorials can provide comfort, preserve memories, and transform grief into a tribute that celebrates the life of your loved one. Whether through planting a garden, establishing a scholarship, designing a plaque, or organizing a remembrance event, these memorials offer a way to keep their spirit alive and find healing.

ENGAGING IN ACTS OF KINDNESS AND SERVICE

Engaging in acts of kindness and service can be a powerful way to navigate grief. When you're grieving, the world can feel incredibly isolating and overwhelming. Acts of kindness, however small, can lift your spirits and create a sense of connection with others. These acts can boost your emotional well-being by shifting your focus from your grief to the positive impact you can have on someone else's life. Engaging in service creates a sense of community and belonging, reminding you that you are not alone. It can also provide a sense of purpose, helping you find meaning and direction in the midst of your loss.

There are many ways to engage in acts of kindness and service. Volunteering at local shelters or food banks is a tangible way to help those in need. These organizations often rely on volunteers to provide meals, sort donations, and offer support to individuals and families facing difficult times. Participating in community clean-up events can also be a fulfilling way to give back. By helping to beautify and maintain public spaces, you contribute to the well-being of your community and create a more pleasant environment for everyone. Random acts of kindness, such as paying for someone's coffee or leaving a cheerful note for a stranger, can brighten someone's day and create a ripple effect of positivity. Donating to causes that were important to your loved one is another meaningful way to honor their memory. Whether it's a local charity, a national organization, or a specific cause they were passionate about, your donation can make a difference and keep their spirit alive.

Consider the story of Sarah, who found healing through acts of kindness after losing her brother. She began volunteering at a local animal shelter, where she spent time caring for abandoned pets. "Seeing the animals thrive and find new homes brought me a sense of joy and purpose," Sarah shared. "It was a way to honor my brother's love for animals and to channel my grief into something positive." Another example is Mark, who organized a community clean-up event in memory of his late wife. "Cleaning up the park where we used to walk together felt like a tribute to her," Mark explained. "The support and participation from friends and neighbors made me feel connected and supported."

Starting your own service project can be a fulfilling way to engage in acts of kindness. Begin by identifying the needs in your community. Perhaps there is a local shelter that could use extra hands, a school that needs supplies, or a public area that could benefit from a clean-up. Once you have identified a need, gather volunteers and resources. Reach out to friends, family, and community members who might be interested in helping. Social media can be a powerful tool for spreading the word and organizing support. Create a project plan and timeline to ensure everything runs smoothly. Outline the tasks that need to be completed, assign roles, and set achievable goals.

For instance, Jane started a project to provide care packages for homeless individuals in her city. She began by researching what items were most needed and reaching out to local shelters for guidance. Jane then gathered a group of friends and family to help collect donations and assemble the packages. "We created a plan and set a date for distribution," Jane said. "Seeing the gratitude on the faces of those we helped was incredibly rewarding. It gave me a sense of purpose and reminded me of the good that can come from even the smallest acts of kindness.

Engaging in acts of kindness and service can be a transformative part of your healing process. By focusing on helping others, you create a sense of connection and purpose that can ease the weight of your grief. Whether through volunteering, random acts of kindness, or starting your own service project, these activities offer a way to channel your emotions into positive action and find moments of joy and fulfillment amidst the pain.

SETTING PERSONAL GOALS FOR HEALING

Setting personal goals can be a powerful tool in the healing process. Goals provide direction and motivation, giving you something to strive for during a time when everything may feel uncertain. They help create a sense of accomplishment and progress, which can be incredibly reassuring when you're navigating grief. Having clear objectives can anchor you, offering a way to focus your energy and efforts constructively. When you set and achieve goals, even small ones, it can boost your confidence and remind you that you can move forward.

One effective technique for setting goals is the SMART method. SMART stands for Specific, Measurable, Achievable, Relevant, and Time-bound. This approach ensures that your goals are clear and attainable, making it easier to track your progress and stay committed. For instance, instead of setting a vague goal like "I want to feel better," a SMART goal would be "I will attend a grief support group once a week for the next three months." This goal is specific, measurable, and time-bound, providing a clear path to follow. Breaking goals into manageable steps can also make them less overwhelming. If your goal is to start a new hobby, begin with small steps like researching classes or gathering materials. Regularly reviewing and adjusting your goals is important. As you progress, you may find that some goals need to be modified, or new ones added.

Incorporating goal-setting exercises into your routine can further support your healing process. Creating a vision board is a visual way to represent your goals and aspirations. Gather images, quotes, and symbols that resonate with you and arrange them on a board. This can serve as a daily reminder of what you're working towards. Goal-setting worksheets can help structure your thoughts and plans. Write down your goals, break them into actionable steps, and set deadlines. Journaling prompts focused on goal reflection can provide clarity and motivation. Questions like "What small steps can I take today towards my goal?" or "What obstacles might I face and how can I overcome them?" can help you stay focused and proactive.

Consider the story of Mike, who lost his mother to a sudden illness. Initially overwhelmed by his grief, Mike decided to set a goal to complete a marathon within a year. He chose this goal because his mother had always encouraged his love for running. Mike broke this goal into smaller steps, starting with short runs and gradually increasing his distance. He used a goal-setting worksheet to track his progress and adjusted his training plan as needed. "Setting this goal gave me something positive to focus on," Mike shared. "Each mile I ran felt like a tribute to my mom." Completing the marathon provided Mike with a profound sense of accomplishment and a way to honor his mother's memory.

Another example is Sarah, who found herself struggling to find purpose after her husband's passing. She set a goal to learn a new language, something she and her husband had always talked about doing together. Sarah used the SMART method to structure her goal, setting specific milestones like completing an online course and practicing with a language partner. She created a vision board with images of the country she wanted to visit and phrases in the new language. "Learning a language became a way to keep our dream alive," Sarah explained. "It gave me a sense of purpose and something to look forward to."

Setting personal goals is crucial for the healing process. They provide direction, motivation, and a sense of accomplishment. Using techniques like SMART goals, breaking them into manageable steps, and regularly reviewing your progress can make goals more attainable. Incorporating exercises like vision board creation, goal-setting worksheets, and journaling prompts can further support your efforts. Personal stories like those of Mike and Sarah illustrate the positive impact that setting and achieving goals can have on your journey through grief.

EMBRACING LIFE AFTER LOSS

After experiencing a profound loss, accepting and embracing a new normal is both challenging and necessary. Life will undoubtedly be different, and understanding this is the first step toward healing. It's important to acknowledge that your life has changed and to find ways to adapt to this new reality. Embracing life after loss means finding joy and meaning in the present moment, even when it feels difficult. This doesn't mean forgetting your loved one or moving on from your grief. Instead, it involves integrating your loss into your life and finding new ways to experience happiness and fulfillment.

To embrace life after loss, consider engaging in new hobbies and interests. Exploring activities that bring you joy can provide a sense of purpose and distraction from your grief. Whether it's painting, cooking, hiking, or learning a new skill, these activities can offer moments of peace and satisfaction. Building new relationships and connections is another important aspect of embracing life. Surround yourself with people who support and understand you. These relationships can provide comfort, companionship, and a sense of belonging. Traveling and exploring new places can also be incredibly healing. Experiencing new environments and cultures can offer a fresh perspective and a break from your daily routine. It's a way to create new memories while honoring the past.

Incorporating exercises for embracing life can help you adjust to your new reality. Gratitude journaling is a powerful tool for shifting your focus to the positive aspects of your life. Each day, write down a few things you are grateful for. This practice can help you recognize the small moments of joy and appreciation that exist even in the midst of grief. Creating a bucket list is another exercise that can bring excitement and motivation. List the activities and experiences you want to have, no matter how big or small. This can give you something to look forward to and work towards. Mindfulness and meditation practices can also aid in embracing life. These practices encourage you to be present and fully engaged with your current experiences. They can help you find calm and clarity, allowing you to appreciate them here and now.

Consider the story of Laura, who lost her husband unexpectedly. Initially, Laura struggled to find joy in life. She decided to take up painting, a hobby she had always been interested in but never pursued. "Painting became my sanctuary," Laura shared. "It gave me a way to express my emotions and find beauty in the world again." Laura also joined a local painting class, where she met new friends who shared her passion. This new community provided her with support and companionship, helping her feel less isolated.

David, who lost his sister, found solace in traveling. He decided to visit the places his sister had always talked about. "Traveling helped me feel closer to her," David explained. "Each new place was a way to honor her memory and create new experiences." David's travels also allowed him to meet new people and experience different cultures, providing a sense of adventure and renewal. Through these stories, it's clear that embracing life after loss is about finding ways to integrate your grief while still moving forward.

As you navigate this new normal, remember to be patient and compassionate with yourself. Embracing life after loss is a gradual process, filled with both challenges and triumphs. By engaging in new hobbies, building relationships, traveling, and incorporating exercises like gratitude journaling and mindfulness, you can find fulfillment and joy once again.

MAKE A DIFFERENCE
UNLOCK THE POWER OF COMFORT AND HEALING

"The best way to find yourself is to lose yourself in the service of others."

MAHATMA GANDHI

Helping others through their hardest times can bring peace and joy into your own life. So, let's make a difference together!

Would you help someone who is struggling with the sudden loss of a loved one? Just like you, they might be searching for answers and a way to heal but not know where to begin.

My goal with *I Didn't Get to Say Goodbye: Healing After the Sudden Death of a Loved One* is to offer comfort, understanding, and practical advice for those going through such a tough time. But to reach more people who need this support, I need your help.

Most people choose books based on reviews. By leaving a review, you could help someone take their first step toward healing after a sudden loss.

It costs nothing and takes only a minute, but your review could make a difference in someone's journey through grief. It could help...

...one more person find hope in their darkest moments.

...one more grieving heart feel understood.

...one more family member heal from the pain of sudden loss.

...one more individual realize they are not alone.

To make a difference, simply scan the QR code below and leave a review:

[https://www.amazon.com/review/review-your-purchases/?asin=BOOKASIN]

If you believe in helping others through tough times, you're my kind of person. Thank you from the bottom of my heart!

Jeffrey Simmons

CONCLUSION

As we come to the end of this book, I want to take a moment to reflect on the journey we've taken together. **I Didn't Get to Say Goodbye: Healing After the Sudden Death of a Loved One** was written with the hope of providing you with the support, practical advice, and emotional comfort you need during one of life's most challenging times. My mission has always been to offer a compassionate companion in your healing journey, helping you navigate the turbulent waters of grief with understanding and empathy.

Throughout these chapters, we've explored the multifaceted nature of grief, recognizing that it is a deeply personal and unique experience for everyone. We started by understanding the various faces of grief and the difference between grief and mourning. We discussed the non-linear nature of the stages of grief and the concept of complicated grief that might need professional help.

We then moved on to the practical aspects of managing daily life amid grief. From prioritizing tasks and setting realistic goals to balancing work and personal responsibilities, we delved into strategies that can help you maintain some semblance of normalcy. We also looked at self-care practices, mindfulness techniques, and the importance of sleep and nutrition in supporting your overall well-being.

In the chapters that followed, we examined coping mechanisms and the importance of emotional support. We talked about journaling, managing unexpected triggers, and dealing with significant dates and anniversaries. We emphasized the value of creating a support network and validating your emotions.

We also shared real-life stories and testimonials to illustrate that you are not alone in your grief. These stories of spousal loss, parental loss, sibling loss, and the loss of friends provided a sense of solidarity and hope. Hearing how others have navigated their grief can offer invaluable insights and encouragement.

Understanding the legal and financial aspects after a sudden death can be overwhelming, so we covered the critical steps to take in the immediate aftermath, managing debts, filing insurance claims, and seeking professional financial advice. These practical steps can provide a sense of structure and purpose during a chaotic time.

We discussed helping children cope with grief, highlighting the importance of honest communication and age-appropriate activities. Supporting a grieving child can be challenging, but it is crucial to provide them with the tools and understanding they need to process their loss.

CONCLUSION

We explored cultural and spiritual perspectives on grief, recognizing that mourning practices vary widely across different cultures and religions. Embracing your cultural heritage and spiritual beliefs can offer profound comfort and a sense of connection during the grieving process.

Finally, we focused on moving forward and finding hope. Building resilience, discovering new purpose and meaning, creating lasting memorials, and engaging in acts of kindness and service were all discussed as ways to navigate life after loss. Setting personal goals and embracing life once again can help you find joy and fulfillment despite the pain of your loss.

As you continue on your journey, remember these key takeaways: Grief is a deeply personal experience, and there is no right or wrong way to navigate it. It's okay to seek help and lean on others for support. Self-care and mindfulness practices can significantly aid in your healing process. Creating lasting memorials and engaging in acts of kindness can provide a sense of purpose and connection. Building resilience and finding new meaning in life are crucial steps in moving forward.

Now, I encourage you to take the next steps in your healing journey. Reach out to support groups, engage in activities that bring you joy, and set small, achievable goals for yourself. Consider creating a memorial for your loved one or participating in community service. These actions can provide comfort and a sense of direction as you navigate your grief.

Remember, healing does not mean forgetting your loved one. It means finding a way to live fully while honoring their memory. Allow yourself to feel the pain, but also give yourself permission to find moments of joy and peace. Your journey through grief is unique, and it's okay to take it one day at a time.

In closing, I want to offer you a heartfelt message of comfort and encouragement. The pain of losing a loved one is profound, and the journey through grief can be long and challenging. But you are not alone. There is a community of people who understand your pain and who are here to support you. Healing is possible, and with time, you will find a way to integrate your loss into your life and move forward with hope and strength.

Thank you for allowing me to be a part of your journey. I hope this book has provided you with the support and comfort you need during this difficult time. Remember, you have the strength within you to heal and find a new path forward. You are not alone, and your loved one's memory will always be a part of you.

Fly high Brittney, I love you.

REFERENCES

What are Normal Physical and Mental Symptoms of Grief? https://www.vitas.com/family-and-caregiver-support/grief-and-bereavement/coping-with-grief/the-normal-physical-and-mental-symptoms-of-grief

Mourning vs. Grief: What's the Difference? - Psych Central https://psychcentral.com/health/mourning-vs-grief

Understanding the five stages of grief https://www.cruse.org.uk/understanding-grief/effects-of-grief/five-stages-of-grief/

Coping With Grief and Loss | National Institute on Aging https://www.nia.nih.gov/health/grief-and-mourning/coping-grief-and-loss

Extreme-Self-Care-on-Your-Grief-Journey.pdf https://www.hospiceandcommunitycare.org/wp-content/uploads/Extreme-Self-Care-on-Your-Grief-Journey.pdf

The Best Task Management Apps for 2024 https://www.pcmag.com/picks/the-best-task-management-apps

Coping With Grief: The Importance of Open Communication https://hopeandhealingforlife.com/2017/12/coping-grief-importance-open-communication/

Mindfulness for Grief and Loss https://www.mindful.org/mindfulness-for-grief-and-loss/

How Journaling Can Help You Grieve https://www.psychologytoday.com/us/blog/understanding-grief/202101/how-journaling-can-help-you-grieve

6 Strategies To Overcome Triggers During Your Grief ... https://www.griefrecoveryhouston.com/strategies-to-overcome-triggers-during-your-grief-recovery/

Coping Strategies for Dates and Days that Make Our Grief Worse https://www.griefandtraumahealing.com/coping-strategies-for-dates-and-days-that-make-our-grief-worse/

Creating a Grief Support Network https://www.memorialutah.com/creating-a-grief-support-network

My first year as a widower: A look at spousal loss and ... https://www.washingtonpost.com/lifestyle/my-first-year-as-a-widower-a-look-at-spousal-loss-and-gradual-recovery/2014/12/29/ce1bc358-7fbc-11e4-81fd-8c4814dfa9d7_story.html

REFERENCES

How to Cope With the Sudden Loss of a Child https://www.parents.com/loss-of-a-child-coping-with-death-8647310

Sibling Grief Club – A community for bereaved siblings. https://siblinggriefclub.com/

Bereavement Intervention Programs https://www.ncbi.nlm.nih.gov/books/NBK217843/

Immediate Steps to Take When a Loved One Dies https://www.unitedway.org/my-smart-money/immediate-needs/a-family-member-has-died/immediate-steps-to-take-when-a-loved-one-dies

How to get a certified copy of a death certificate https://www.usa.gov/death-certificate

The Probate Process - American Bar Association https://www.americanbar.org/groups/real_property_trust_estate/resources/estate-planning/probate-process

How do I file a life insurance claim? | III https://www.iii.org/article/how-do-i-file-life-insurance-claim

Developmental Manifestations of Grief in Children and ... https://www.ncbi.nlm.nih.gov/pmc/articles/PMC8794619/

How to talk to your children about the death of a loved one https://www.unicef.org/parenting/child-care/how-talk-your-children-about-death-loved-one

7 Touching Books to Help Kids Understand Death and Grief https://www.scholastic.com/parents/books-and-reading/raise-a-reader-blog/7-touching-books-to-help-kids-understand-death-and-grief.html

National Alliance for Children's Grief https://nacg.org/

Day of the Dead - Wikipedia https://en.wikipedia.org/wiki/Day_of_the_Dead

How to Prepare a Gospel-Centered Funeral When You're ... https://churchsource.com/blogs/ministry-resources/how-to-prepare-a-gospel-centered-funeral-when-youre-under-pressure

Grief and Buddhism: Comfort in Impermanence https://whatsyourgrief.com/grief-and-buddhism-comfort-in-impermanence/

Japanese Traditions: Obon https://www.jcchawaii.org/resources/obon

Resilience Psychology and Coping with Grief https://drarielleschwartz.com/resilience-psychology-and-coping-with-grief/

How to Find Purpose In Life After Experiencing Profound Grief https://transitionandthrivewithmaria.com/how-to-find-purpose-in-life-after-experiencing-profound-grief/

11 Best Memorial Ideas for Loss of Your Loved Ones https://www.eterneva.com/resources/memorialize-loved-ones

The Mental Health Benefits of Simple Acts of Kindness https://www.psychiatry.org/news-room/apa-blogs/mental-health-benefits-simple-acts-of-kindness